RESOLVING HEDDA

Jon Klein

BROADWAY PLAY PUBLISHING INC
New York
www.broadwayplaypub.com
info@broadwayplaypub.com

RESOLVING HEDDA
© Copyright 2018 Jon Klein

Cover art by Jennifer Logan

First edition: September 2018
I S B N: 978-0-88145-795-7

Book design: Marie Donovan
Page make-up: Adobe InDesign
Typeface: Palatino

RESOLVING HEDDA was first produced in an extended run by The Victory Theatre Center (produced by Maria Gobetti, Tom Ormeny, and Katie Witkowski) in Burbank, California from 29 September to 3 December 2017. The cast and creative contributors were:

HEDDA.. Kimberly Alexander
AUNT JULIA ....Alyce Heath
GEORGE ....Ben Atkinson
THEA... Marisa Van Den Borre
BRACK...Tom Ormeny
EILERT.. Chad Coe
STAGEHAND .... Sean Spencer

Director.. Maria Gobetti
Set design.. Evan Bartoletti
Lighting design .... Carol Doehring
Costume design................................... A Jeffrey Schoenberg
Sound design...Noah Andrade
Prop design .... Gigi Palacio

The play won the 2018 Michael Devereaux Award in Los Angeles for Best Playwriting of the 2017 theater season.

CHARACTERS & SETTING

HEDDA, *mid 20s*
AUNT JULIA, *60s*
GEORGE, *early 30s*
THEA, *mid 20s*
BRACK, *mid 40s*
EILERT, *early 30s*

There is also a STAGEHAND, *who occasionally makes an appearance, but has no lines.*

Oslo, Norway

SCENES

ACT ONE:

Scene One—Morning
Scene Two—That Evening

ACT TWO:

Scene One—Next Morning
Scene Two—That Evening

DESIGN ELEMENTS

The set design and costumes (with notable exceptions) can and should be for any traditional production of HEDDA GABLER, whether elaborate or minimalist. Check Ibsen's stage description for more information, if you wish. Essential furniture includes a couch, a few chairs, a writing desk and a cabinet.

NOTE ON THIS PLAY

There are no actors in this play. Only the characters, who know their dramatic functions intrinsically, and have been used to fulfilling them in certain ways. That changes now.

SYNOPSIS OF *HEDDA GABLER* (THE OTHER PLAY)

Henrik Ibsen's play *Hedda Gabler* premiered in Munich in 1891, with subsequent productions the same year in Berlin, Copenhagen and London. When the play begins, Hedda—the beautiful but willful daughter of a famous general—has just returned from a honeymoon with her academic husband, Georges Tesman. Soon after their return, Hedda is reacquainted with an old school friend, Thea Elvsted, as well as the brilliant but wayward writer Eilert Lovborg. Hedda is bored and frustrated with her new life, as well as jealous of Thea's comparative freedom. So she finds pleasure by coming between them, manipulating Lovborg into drinking again and convincing him to take his own life with one of her father's pistols. She also burns Lovborg's only manuscript of his new book (which Tesman had found discarded on the street). However, Hedda finds herself under the control of their imposing friend, Judge Brack, who makes it clear that he knows she gave Lovborg the gun. Trapped and threatened with exposure, Hedda retreats to an adjoining room and kills herself with the second pistol.

ACT ONE

Scene One

(Any preshow announcement, if there is one, is interrupted by the sudden appearance of HEDDA *onstage. She pushes the announcer offstage and addresses the audience. House lights dim slightly, if at all.)*

HEDDA: Don't take pictures, unwrap your candy now, turn off your cell phones. Blah, blah, blah. Unimportant. These things don't matter. As a matter of fact, it wouldn't be a bad idea for a few of you to keep your phones on and ready to use—at least on airplane mode. And yes, I know what an airplane is. I know a lot of stuff that might surprise you.

For example…by the end of this show, unless something goes wrong—or should I say right… anyway, there's going to be a murder. That's why your cell phones might prove handy. To call 911, when it happens. And it always does. It always has. How do I know? I'm the murder victim. I've been the victim over ten thousand times, ever since this fucking play was first produced in 1891. Sorry for the spoiler alert—but that's what you paid for. I die at the end of the play. Shot through the head. Kablam. Of course I die. People love to see me die. They can't wait for it. They can't get enough of it.

I should clarify. I'm not talking about the actress playing me, whoever she is. She's a nice person, I'm sure, they usually are. Thrilled to get a lead role for a change, especially one for which she doesn't have to take off her clothes. But she doesn't have a clue about what it all means to *me*. She doesn't have to die. She gets to come back for the next show and do the same tortured crap every night till the curtain falls. Then she goes out with the cast to the dive down the street, eats a late night Cobb salad, flirts a little with the guy playing Eilert, just to stay in character, maybe even has a glass of chardonnay if she's feeling good about herself. Meanwhile, I'm left on the floor, bleeding. Fake blood for her—but real blood for me. Get it? The character—that's me, Hedda G—dies. Every stinking night. Sometimes offstage, sometimes in full view. Depends on the director's taste for shock value. But whether you see it or not, I always get shot in the head. With my own pistol.

Lemme ask you something, out of professional curiosity. Any of you ever been shot? No? Didn't think so. Theatregoers—wrong demographic. So let me tell you a little something about bullets. They hurt. Like a son of a bitch. Even when they enter the brain. Sure, it may only last a second or two, but now imagine thousands and thousands of them, over a period of a hundred years and more. Sometimes dozens in one night, all around the world. Sure, I may be speaking in other languages, but bullets don't require much translation, know what I mean? I die and I die and I die and I die and I die and—I've *had* it.

Another spoiler. Those of you who know this play are already saying, hold on babe, you're talking about murder, but that's not how it ends—nobody whacks you. You blow out your own brains—nobody does it for you. So who are you to blame anyone else on what's essentially a matter of poor decision making? Well, I hear you, Jack, but think again. It's murder, and

I'll tell you who the murderer is. No big secret. His
name is Ibsen. *(She calls offstage.)* Hey—does anybody
have some water back there? All this monologuing is
giving me dry mouth.

(A sheepish STAGEHAND *comes out wearing earphones, with
a bottle of water.)*

HEDDA: Oh, look at this. Deer in the headlights.
Wondering what to do. "Has she gone bonkers
already? That doesn't happen for four more acts."
Thanks, kid. You may now return to whatever
indentured servitude was arranged for you.

(The STAGEHAND *runs off.* HEDDA *drinks.)*

HEDDA: Ahh. That's better. Where was I? Oh yeah.
Ibsen. The Norwegian serial killer. Could have been a
pharmacist, but he chose the theatre. You'd be amazed
how many playwrights say that on a daily basis, by
the way. Had a baby when he was eighteen, never
saw the kid after the birth, but paid child support
until it turned fourteen. Make of that what you
psychologically will. Let's see, what else about Ibsy?
Lived in relative obscurity and poverty most of his
life, had some regional success in Scandinavia—the
equivalent of having a hit play in—oh, let's say...
Indianapolis.

Fast forward to 1891. Good ol' Ibsy is about sixty-two,
and quite famous. He even has a flock of young female
admirers—ack, urg, sorry, my gag reflex—I'm okay
now. So at the peak of his fame and popularity, for
some unknown reason he decides to create the perfect
killing machine—this play, starring yours truly. The
foolproof entrapment of an independently minded
woman at the end of the nineteenth century, assailed
by all sides and thwarted at every turn, until she
has no choice but to off herself. That's murder in my
book. And by the way, this guy Ibsen? Most respected

centers of learning call him the first male "feminist."
Oh, sure. Creating the circumstances in which a
woman is forced to kill herself. Myself, I don't call that
feminism. I call it gaslighting. Know what that means?
It comes from yet another play. And played by Ingrid
Bergman in the movie version. Come to think of it,
she played me too. Huh. Tell you what. Let's all take a
moment of silence to reflect on the inspirational life of
Ingrid Bergman. *(She closes her eyes.)*

(Lights shift.)

*(AUNT JULIA enters, confused. She wears a large, oddly
designed hat.)*

JULIA: Hedda?

HEDDA: Do you mind? I'm kinda in the *middle* of
something here.

JULIA: I thought you'd still be in bed. Where's Berta?

(HEDDA turns to look at JULIA.)

HEDDA: Ah. Aunt Julie. Of course. It's begun.

JULIA: What's begun?

HEDDA: The play.

JULIA: What play? I don't understand what you're
referring to.

HEDDA: I'm sure you don't. Never mind. I let Berta go
today.

JULIA: You dismissed her?

HEDDA: Naw. Just gave her a personal day. She's not
that essential to the plot.

JULIA: I'm very confused. *(She removes her hat and puts it
in a conspicuous place.)*

HEDDA: As usual. Please don't put that there. It looks
like something crawled there and died.

JULIA: But Hedda, I just bought it! For your arrival!

HEDDA: Whatever for? This isn't Halloween. I suggest you get your money back—if you can. Maybe it was still breathing when they sold it to you.

JULIA: Have I done something to offend you? If so, I hope you will inform me so I can make amends.

HEDDA: Oh, God. No one has time for that kind of exposition. *(Pause. She catches herself.)* Wait. I'm forgetting the cardinal rule of Stanislavski—the illusion of the first time. Note to self. If I act like I've done this before, I lose all interest.

JULIA: I'm sorry? What—

HEDDA: No, I'm the one who's sorry. What were you saying, Aunt Julie? Something about Berta?

JULIA: Well, if she *were* here, I would have reassured her about working here, instead of for me and my sister.

HEDDA: Want her back? She's yours.

JULIA: Heavens no. She's much needed here.

HEDDA: For what? Dusting the furniture? Making tea? Announcing the guests? Like some reject from Downton Abbey?

JULIA: I'm not familiar with—

HEDDA: Never mind. Really, take her back if you like. There won't be much need for her services around here.

JULIA: What about George?

HEDDA: I see your point, he is pretty useless. But really, he's going to have to learn to do a few things for himself. Polish his own shoes, occasionally take out the garbage—

JULIA: But will he have the time? He just received his doctorate, and I know my own nephew well enough to know he can't handle trivial distractions.

HEDDA: Oh, give me a break. He could use a few distractions. I can't even give the guy a handjob without him reaching for a notebook.

JULIA: I'm sorry, what did you give him?

HEDDA: How long did his mother breast feed him? Till he was five?

JULIA: Six, actually. It was prescribed for his colic.

HEDDA: My point exactly. You're not his mother, and I'm not his maid. He's going to have to get his head out of the books and pitch in around here.

(GEORGE *enters, carrying a large stack of books and manuscripts.*)

GEORGE: Aunt Julie! Just look at the research materials I accumulated on our trip!

JULIA: George—

GEORGE: Old manuscripts, first editions, rare reprints—I used every spare moment tearing through the great libraries of Europe.

HEDDA: Yes. It was quite a honeymoon.

(GEORGE *drops the books, startled.*)

GEORGE: Hedda! What in the world are you doing here?

HEDDA: I believe I live here. At least that's what you told me last night when you brought me here.

GEORGE: I mean, what are you doing out of bed? Already? This is…unusual.

HEDDA: I suppose it is. Tell you what. Get used to the unexpected.

JULIA: Hedda is very different today, George. One might say, out of sorts.

GEORGE: Where's Berta? Berta!

JULIA: She's been dismissed.

GEORGE: Dismissed? By whom?

HEDDA: By me, George. We're not helpless. This is the...which is it, 19th? —century. We can defrost our own dinners.

JULIA: You see what I mean.

GEORGE: Are you feeling well this morning, darling?

HEDDA: Better than ever.

GEORGE: But your manner is—

HEDDA: Completely normal. I want to live, George. Do you understand what I'm saying? I don't want to die.

GEORGE: Well...I think we're all in agreement there, my fretful little sparrow.

HEDDA: Ack. George. Let's get something straight if we're going to get along for the next hundred and fifty years or so. Don't ever call me that again. Or your kitten, your pet, your cupcake, your sweetie, your better half, your little peach cheeks, your little kumquat, your little cabbage, or anything else with the word "little" in front of it. Let's just be safe and stay away from all terms of endearment, foreign or domestic. Call me Hedda. Just don't call me late for dinner. *(Pause)* Oh, come on. Not even a giggle? That joke is *ancient*. I bet Aunt Julie's heard it.

JULIA: Certainly not. I don't even understand it.

GEORGE: Hedda, I am exceedingly concerned about you. I'm wondering if you shouldn't go back to bed. The ill effects of the trip are still affecting you.

JULIA: Ill effects?

GEORGE: Yes, I'm afraid my poor wife was feeling a bit queasy this morning.

JULIA: Queasy?

HEDDA: Oh for God's sake, let's call it what it was. I puked. A perfectly normal bodily function. Especially after five months on the road. I probably had a bad chimichanga in the Yucatan.

GEORGE: But this wasn't just the one time, Hedda. You've had some level of illness several mornings while we were away.

JULIA: In the mornings, eh?

HEDDA: I know where you're going with this, Aunt Julie. Nothing could be further from the truth.

JULIA: Perhaps.

GEORGE: I'm afraid I don't quite comprehend.

HEDDA: Yes, thank God you're so thick-headed, George. It's probably your most endearing quality.

GEORGE: Why, Hedda, I'm flattered!

HEDDA: Exactly. Let's get back on track, shall we? Ask Julie about Aunt Rina.

GEORGE: Heavens, yes! How is your poor sister today?

JULIA: Thank you for asking—eventually. Her time is short, I'm afraid. But she is so grateful to have me there.

HEDDA: I'm curious, Aunt Julie. What exactly is her malady?

JULIA: She's very ill.

HEDDA: Yes, I understand that. But in all this time, I've never understood from what. Heart disease? Parkinsons? Diabetes? Osteoporosis? Incontinence? What?

GEORGE: Why, Hedda, I had no idea you were so informed about such things! Have you been reading medical books in your spare time?

JULIA: I'm not sure what some of those words mean.

HEDDA: Has she even been to see a doctor?

JULIA: Of course. He told her it's only natural to feel poorly at her age.

HEDDA: Really. Where did this genius get his degree? Online?

GEORGE: What are you suggesting, Hedda?

HEDDA: I'm suggesting that with a real diagnosis, there might be a treatment or two that would be more helpful than Julie's chicken soup.

JULIA: She looks forward to my soup!

HEDDA: I'm sure she does. It's also nice of you to change her bedpans, but I don't think that can prolong anybody's life.

GEORGE: Try to be gentle, Hedda.

HEDDA: It's common sense, George. Aunt Rina needs a specialist. Otherwise, I promise you, she's going to be room temperature by tomorrow.

JULIA: What!

GEORGE: Hedda! I think you owe Aunt Julie an apology.

HEDDA: You're right, that was insensitive. I'm just tired of all this foreshadowing.

GEORGE: Perhaps you should lie down.

HEDDA: I'm serious. Why do our daily conversations have to fit in with some old Norwegian's sense of dramatic structure?

GEORGE: I'm at a loss as to what's going on with you today.

JULIA: Yes, go back to bed. You're not even supposed to be here. Berta's supposed to be here!

HEDDA: I can see I've become quite an irritant. I'll just head downstage and read about the actress playing me. *(She comes down to the front row and points to a patron's program.)* Can I borrow that? *(She takes the program and reads it near the audience.)*

GEORGE: I forgot what I wanted to discuss…

HEDDA: *(Not looking up)* Your prospects?

GEORGE: Oh, yes, my prospects!

JULIA: Have you heard about your professorship?

GEORGE: Not officially, but I've been told my chances are favorable. It's between myself and…oh, what's that fellow's name? The radical philosopher? With the passionate disposition?

HEDDA: Don't forget his sexual magnetism.

GEORGE: Yes, I suppose so. Do you know the man, Hedda?

HEDDA: Eilert Lovborg.

GEORGE: Yes, that's the one!

HEDDA: Never heard of him.

GEORGE: Ah. Well. Lovborg does have a few supporters. So I can't count my chickens quite yet.

JULIA: Maybe you can. Lovborg became quite a scandalous figure for several years. For decorum's sake, I won't sully the atmosphere by mentioning the nature of his shocking behavior.

HEDDA: Booze and prostitutes.

(They turn to stare at HEDDA.*)*

JULIA: Apparently so. I daresay the university wouldn't risk hiring someone with his reputation.

GEORGE: That is a relief. Not for poor Eilert, of course.

HEDDA: Of course.

JULIA: Though I probably should mention...

HEDDA: Wait for it...

JULIA: He seems to have written a new book.

HEDDA: And there it is.

GEORGE: A new book? What's it about?

JULIA: Well, as far as I could tell, it's a reexamination of the history of the world, establishing newly realized connections between cultural, religious and political trends and revolutions, leading to detailed analyses of current socio-economic factors. Anyway, that's the rumor.

GEORGE: Good lord.

JULIA: But I'm sure that pales in comparison to the topic of your latest endeavor. What's it about, again?

GEORGE: The Landgraviate of Brabant.

JULIA: I see.

GEORGE: Specifically, the year 1085, when it was annexed after the death of the Count of Lotharingia. *(Pause)* I may expand on that.

JULIA: No need, I'm sure.

HEDDA: *(To the audience)* This is the kind of stuff they talk about when I'm not in the room.

GEORGE: What was that, Hedda?

HEDDA: Nothing. *(She hands the program back to the patron.)* Thanks. She sounds fantastic. *(She wanders back upstage.)*

GEORGE: I think our trip agreed with my new wife, Aunt Julie. Don't you think she has filled out marvelously?

JULIA: Filled out, you say!

HEDDA: What are you saying, George? You think I'm fat?

GEORGE: No! Not at all!

HEDDA: I wouldn't be surprised, the way you insisted on eating at the hotel restaurants. I would have killed for an occasional Jamba Juice.

JULIA: I think George is saying something entirely different, Hedda.

HEDDA: Oh yeah? What's that, George?

GEORGE: Umm…just that you look…quite healthy?

HEDDA: Meaning what?

GEORGE: Well, you seem to have gained… Damn. Let me start over.

JULIA: I think he's alluding to the possibility that you may have some exciting news, Hedda. Do you have anything you'd like to share?

HEDDA: Oh, Jesus, Julie. Once and for all, can't you take your grotesque headgear and hit the road? I'm sure George will give you a call when he needs his nose wiped.

GEORGE: Hedda!

JULIA: It's all right, George. A woman in her condition is prone to emotional instability.

GEORGE: Condition?

HEDDA: Yes, I have a condition. The reason for my morning nausea, as well as my general irritability. I suppose I should go ahead and say it out loud.

JULIA: Oh, please do, Hedda! Say the words we're longing to hear!

HEDDA: Very well. Irritable bowel syndrome.

JULIA: What?

HEDDA: Commonly known as diarrhea.

GEORGE: I'm not sure I was longing to hear those words.

JULIA: As you wish, Hedda. Goodbye, nephew.

GEORGE: I will come to see Aunt Rina later today, I promise.

JULIA: I pray your wife will be more like herself, the next time I see her. *(She grabs her hat and storms out.)*

GEORGE: Honestly, Hedda! Why were you so rude to that sweet old woman? I love you so, but sometimes I wonder about you.

HEDDA: Do you, George? Love me?

GEORGE: Of course I do.

HEDDA: Why do you? I'm relatively pretty, I suppose—

GEORGE: Pretty? Why, you're lovely beyond description! Certainly the most beautiful woman within the immediate geographical area—

HEDDA: Quit while you're ahead, George. Aside from my stunning beauty, what features do I possess that make you love me so? I'm bored, willful and perverse. At least according to Wikipedia.

GEORGE: I don't know what you mean.

HEDDA: It's a simple question. Why do you love me?

GEORGE: *(Exasperated)* Because…I…just do. What kinds of questions are these? *(He looks toward the door.)* I better catch up with Aunt Julie and apologize for your behavior. She's quite right. You simply are not yourself today. *(He exits.)*

*(*HEDDA *pauses, disturbed. She turns to the audience.)*

HEDDA: That's not quite true. I always take my personal frustrations out on that harmless old busybody. The real question is—why do I do it? What if I'm not really a bad person—I've just been *written* that way? Why do I let someone with sideburns the size of Florida dictate all my actions? What if I just *refuse* to go along with it? My God—I could change the actual course of the play. And I could live! *(Her demeanor changes.)* But how? Ibsen has me locked into so many inescapable plot points that Houdini himself couldn't find a way out. I'd have to—go against my own nature. Become a completely different person. I'd have to…care more about other people, and less about myself. I wonder—could I do that? Maybe I could! That doesn't have to be so hard. Just thinking about it makes me cheerier, more hopeful, makes me want to… *(She runs offstage, covering her mouth.)*

*(*THEA *enters from the opposite side, looking around.)*

THEA: Hello? Hedda? *(She looks at a small bouquet of flowers, and examines the card with it.)* She hasn't even read this yet!

*(*HEDDA *returns to the room, carrying a tin of breath mints.)*

HEDDA: Hello, Thea. Would you like an Altoid? They're curiously strong.

THEA: Hedda Gabler! You don't even seem surprised to see me!

HEDDA: Well, I've pretty much memorized the sequence.

THEA: What?

HEDDA: I mean—the flowers! I found your flowers, announcing your arrival! How kind of you to let me know you were coming.

THEA: The card was unopened.

HEDDA: Well then—Thea! Oh my God! I'm utterly shocked to see you here!

THEA: You are?

HEDDA: Absolutely. I mistook you for Thea Goldstein. Ladies' Auxiliary. But of course now I recognize you— Thea Elvsted! How long has it been since we've seen each other!

THEA: Not since we were in school, I think.

HEDDA: Yes, you were the cutest little tease, weren't you? All the boys were obsessed with your fantastic blonde hair.

THEA: Are you making fun of me?

HEDDA: Me? Make fun of you? The head cheerleader?

THEA: I'm not sure what a cheerleader is. But as I remember, the boys came to you for *your* head.

(Pause. HEDDA is taken aback.)

HEDDA: Excuse me?

THEA: You had such a regal profile. Like Cleopatra herself. You had many more admirers than me.

HEDDA: That's true. But you were no slouch in the heartbreaker department, Thea. Let's just agree that we're both uncommonly hot.

THEA: If you say so.

HEDDA: I do. So what brings you here from the wasteland, Thea? Any news you'd like to share? About anyone in particular?

THEA: Well yes, though it's a bit awkward and I will need several minutes to explain.

HEDDA: Oh, Christ. Do you really? I'm hoping to get this show down to two acts.

(GEORGE *enters.*)

GEORGE: Aunt Julie was very forgiving. My word! Is this who I think it is?

THEA: Hello, Mr Tesman.

GEORGE: Oh, please, not so formal. We did know each other once, you know.

HEDDA: That's right, you two used to be quite a number.

GEORGE: That was long before I met you, Hedda. Please call me George, Mrs Elvsted. You are, I believe, still married to the Sheriff of that little town near the college.

THEA: Yes, but really, you must call me Thea.

HEDDA: Good God, this could go on for hours. Thea has come with some news about Eilert Lovborg.

THEA: Hedda! How could you possibly know that? I haven't said a thing about him.

HEDDA: Apparently he's here in town, and Thea followed him here. (*She turns to* THEA.) Oh, don't be so shocked. Word gets around. This town is a regular Peyton Place. (*She turns to the audience.*) I know, old reference for some of you.

THEA: Well, I'm afraid Hedda's…incredibly blunt summation is true. I'm hoping to find Eilert before something terrible happens to him.

HEDDA: Then let's make it a point not to let anything terrible happen.

THEA: How kind of you, Hedda!

HEDDA: Believe me, it would be best for all involved.

GEORGE: I don't understand. This is too fast for me.

HEDDA: Just go with it, George.

GEORGE: But how do you know Eilert Lovborg?

THEA: He was my children's tutor.

GEORGE: Ah. So you have children?

HEDDA: Can we stay on topic? This is a really pointless detour.

THEA: It's all right, Hedda. I don't mind explaining.

HEDDA: I know you don't. That's the problem.

THEA: I have two step-children. Eilert was kind enough to teach them basic reading and writing.

HEDDA: While he taught you biology. Am I right?

THEA: I'm not sure I care for your insinuations, Hedda.

HEDDA: Insinuations? I think I'm being pretty damn clear about it. Really, doing it with the babysitter? What a cliché. I'm surprised he didn't deliver pizza.

GEORGE: You must excuse Hedda. She's having an unusually candid day.

HEDDA: Perhaps I should be equally candid. About my own previous relationship with Eilert.

GEORGE: What's this? I thought you didn't know him.

HEDDA: Oh, no big deal. I met him once at some club after graduation. We exchanged phone numbers, but he never called. Kind of a nerd, really. Thea, I can't get over how beautifully you've maintained your hair. Makes you look no older than thirty.

THEA: I'm twenty-seven.

HEDDA: That was my next guess. I tell you, it's the hair. I'm all about your hair.

THEA: You used to call it a haystack.

HEDDA: And you didn't hear that as a compliment? I'm shocked. I would love to have haystack hair, any day.

GEORGE: I'm still confused. About Eilert.

HEDDA: We've moved on, George.

GEORGE: Did you find his behavior trustworthy? I've heard some rather unseemly stories.

THEA: He has sworn off all vices and has been living an exemplary life for the last two years.

HEDDA: That's a shame. I mean, good for you. I'm sure it was your positive influence.

THEA: I like to think so, yes.

HEDDA: As well as your hair.

THEA: But he became so restless after his book was published.

GEORGE: Oh yes, his book. You've seen it, then?

THEA: I read every word. It's the most brilliant thing I've ever read in my life.

GEORGE: Oh. That's…splendid. Well, it's been good to see you, Thea.

THEA: Please don't go, Mr Tesman.

GEORGE: George.

THEA: George. I have a favor to ask you.

HEDDA: I'm not sure that's going to be a good idea.

GEORGE: Let her make her request, Hedda.

THEA: I'm worried that Eilert may fall into some old… bad habits. Now that he's in the big city.

HEDDA: You mean the booze and prostitutes?

(THEA *bursts into tears.*)

GEORGE: Hedda! Stop that! Can't you see Mrs Elvsted is distraught?

THEA: You must befriend him if he comes here! And watch out for him, keep him safe. He considers you such a good friend!

GEORGE: Does he really?

THEA: Yes, from the old days. He admires your scholarship!

(HEDDA *has a coughing fit, to cover her laughter.*)

GEORGE: Well, that's very kind of him. I also consider him an intellectual peer.

(HEDDA *has another fit.*)

HEDDA: Sorry!

GEORGE: If he comes, I will certainly do what I can.

THEA: Thank you.

(*Pause.* GEORGE *and* THEA *both look at* HEDDA.)

THEA: Umm…Hedda?

HEDDA: Yes? What is it?

THEA: You know.

HEDDA: No I don't.

THEA: Weren't you going to suggest something?

HEDDA: I don't think so.

THEA: Perhaps you were going to suggest that George write Eilert a letter.

GEORGE: Were you now, Hedda?

THEA: Yes. To invite him here to your house. To assess his situation. And offer him friendship.

GEORGE: Why, that's a capital idea, Hedda! How kind and generous of you!

THEA: And perhaps I can meet him here after he arrives.

GEORGE: Even better. I'll write him at once! *(He exits.)*

HEDDA: I really don't think that's necessary, Thea. As a matter of fact, I'm not sure Eilert should come here at all.

THEA: Why ever not?

HEDDA: It might send things into motion. A series of events that will be hard for me to stop, once it begins. Having to do with vine leaves, book burning and…hair pulling! *(She tugs on THEA's hair.)*

THEA: Ow! What are you doing!

(HEDDA lets go.)

HEDDA: Sorry. I mean it. I'm very sorry. I think I must have I C D.

THEA: I C D?

HEDDA: Impulse control disorder. It's a common malady among female characters. Emma Bovary, Anna Karenina, Scarlett O'Hara, Mary Poppins, you name it.

THEA: I don't know these women.

HEDDA: Nor should you. You have a pure heart, Thea. Not even a hint of deception or manipulation, and I congratulate you for that. You don't even have the slightest fear of scandal, which is why you've been able to bump uglies with Eilert Lovborg without any worries.

THEA: Hedda! How can you say such things!

HEDDA: Rather easily, it seems.

THEA: Word games. You always loved to play these kinds of word games, even back in school. Thank heavens I learned not to take you seriously. Otherwise I would be very cross with you.

HEDDA: As I remember, you got plenty cross with me. Especially when I...pulled your hair! *(She pulls* THEA's *hair again.)*

THEA: Stop that! What's wrong with you?

*(*THEA *slaps* HEDDA's *hand away.)*

HEDDA: I told you—I C D. Believe me, I don't like it any more than you do.

(Pause)

*(*HEDDA *reaches for her hair again, but* THEA *slaps it away in time.)*

HEDDA: Sorry.

THEA: I suppose I must be going.

HEDDA: Nonsense. You came here to spill the beans about your infidelity, and you haven't even gotten started.

THEA: That's not true.

HEDDA: Let's skip the next ten minutes of denial, shall we? I'll lay it out for you. You went to work as a governess for Wyatt Earp, or his Norwegian counterpart, and married this guy when his wife died from boredom or syphilis she probably contracted from her husband, am I right? And he was what, fifteen years older than you?

THEA: Twenty.

HEDDA: Twenty. Sheesh. So your husband Pat Garrett, or his Norwegian counterpart, spent all his time on the road tracking down Billy the Kid, or his Norwegian counterpart, and left you in the hands of a sexy writer philosopher babysitter who has no counterpart to speak of.

THEA: I suppose.

HEDDA: So who could blame you for falling in love? Not I. And certainly not me.

THEA: You're very understanding.

HEDDA: You're not worried about Sheriff Lobo sending out a posse to find you?

THEA: I don't care if he does. I'm not going back there.

HEDDA: Really? You're not worried about the press? Paparazzi? Anything?

THEA: I'm not ashamed of anything.

HEDDA: That's remarkable, Thea. I could never be that way.

THEA: I know. You can't even tell your husband about your own past with Eilert.

HEDDA: What past? It was just a couple of encounters, nothing more.

THEA: Thirty-seven, to be exact. He kept a journal. Which I read.

HEDDA: Oh. Did he mention that time with the—

THEA: Yes.

HEDDA: When we were in the middle of the—

THEA: Yes. There are no secrets between us.

HEDDA: Damn his journalistic instincts. I want you to know, I don't do that kind of thing any more.

THEA: I don't see how you could.

HEDDA: Good.

THEA: How *anyone* could. Logistically.

HEDDA: All right then. So here's the thing. I'll admit it to you. I'm jealous. You have more power over Eilert Lovborg than I ever could. My hat's off to you.

THEA: Well, I wouldn't call it power, exactly. Just because I got him to give up the drinking, and the... the...

HEDDA: Prostitutes.

THEA: Yes, those. And just because I influenced him to write the most important book of the modern age. I wouldn't call that power. I'd call it...you know, you're right, let's call it power. I like that. Power. Eilert is *under my power*—

HEDDA: Don't brag about it. So far this scene doesn't even pass the Bechdel test.

THEA: The what?

HEDDA: Here's what you need to know. I don't want him here. I'm not as strong as you, Thea. Not as noble. I'm a weak person. And if Eilert comes here, I may not have the will to keep things on the right track. I tend to cause trouble. And in this case, trouble could have horrible results—for him, for you and for me. I don't want that any more. I can't imagine why I ever did.

THEA: Probably the—what is it again? —I C D?

HEDDA: Yes, exactly! You understand!

THEA: I may not trust you, Hedda Gabler, but I trust Eilert. I trust him implicitly. We have a bond that goes deeper than mere physical attraction.

HEDDA: Come off it, Thea. You're not in high school.

THEA: Although...there is rumor of another woman from his past. Someone he may have loved.

HEDDA: The rumors are true. Believe me.

THEA: Some sort of...singer.

HEDDA: Singer? I don't know about that. I mean, I used to try the occasional karaoke bar.

THEA: Not you. A redhead.

HEDDA: That's right—the redhead.

THEA: This person—this woman—seems to have acquired a rather scandalous reputation. I don't want him to find her.

HEDDA: I don't blame you. Chlamydia is not a flower.

THEA: So you can see why I'm anxious to find him.

HEDDA: Certainly. But I'm telling you it's a mistake to have him come here.

THEA: I don't think so.

HEDDA: You can't possibly be that naïve.

THEA: I'm not a virgin.

HEDDA: That's a relief.

THEA: At least not over and over. Like some women I know.

HEDDA: Is that supposed to refer to me?

THEA: If the shoe fits. See? I can do word games too!

HEDDA: Here's another game. One that's very popular among young girls. *(She grabs a candle and approaches* THEA.*)* Let's burn Barbie's hair off!

*(*THEA *shrieks and runs offstage, frightened.)*

*(*HEDDA *stops, realizing what she's doing, and puts down the candle.)*

HEDDA: Oh man. Déjà vu. Why do I always end up doing that? I'm playing right into Ibsen's hands. And I'll wind up dead on the stage floor. This will take a lot more concentration than I realized. I have to ignore my own instincts.

*(*JUDGE BRACK *calls from offstage.)*

BRACK: *(Offstage)* Hello? Mrs Tesman?

HEDDA: Perfect example.

(BRACK *enters as* HEDDA *turns to him.*)

HEDDA: Judge Brack.

BRACK: My dear Mrs Tesman! How wonderful to see you again!

HEDDA: How does this usually go? We do a lot of harmless flirtation, just for the fun of it. But that doesn't turn out so harmless in the end, does it?

BRACK: Mrs Tesman?

HEDDA: Just a minute, Judge. I'm talking to the audience.

BRACK: What?

HEDDA: See, eventually, he'll be in a position to blackmail me. And that won't do. Maybe if I'm more encouraging? I could ramp things up, give him a little more hope. That might turn things in a whole new direction. Yes, I think I'll try that. (*She turns to him.*) How are you today, Judge?

BRACK: You spoke of an audience. Are you rehearsing some sort of play?

HEDDA: Indeed I am. How perceptive of you.

BRACK: I'm relieved to hear it. I was about to have my doubts.

HEDDA: Oh, I'm the same old fun loving girl you always hope for.

BRACK: Really? And how is that, pray tell?

HEDDA: However you prefer, Judge. On the couch? Out on the verandah? Or should we just go downtown and rent a room for a few hours?

BRACK: (*Confused*) Why, Mrs Tesman. I believe you're teasing me.

HEDDA: Sure, I can do that too, if that's what you're into. I missed your company while I was gone on that pointless trip.

BRACK: Pointless? That was your honeymoon.

HEDDA: Exactly.

BRACK: Mrs Tesman. I believe you've become even more of a minx than before, if such a thing is possible.

HEDDA: Oh, it's possible, Judgy. Highly possible. (*She grabs his ass as she passes him.*)

(BRACK *reacts with astonishment as* GEORGE *enters the room, carrying a letter.*)

GEORGE: Judge Brack! What a pleasure to see you after our long journey!

(BRACK *is still staring at* HEDDA.)

GEORGE: Judge? Hello?

BRACK: Oh, yes, my dear fellow. I wanted to be the first to welcome you back.

GEORGE: Thank you.

BRACK: I entered unannounced. For some reason Berta didn't answer the door.

GEORGE: Yes, she's gone.

BRACK: Gone?

GEORGE: It's a long story. But since she's not here, I'll have to be the one to post this letter. I'll return momentarily. Hedda, can you find a way to entertain our friend the Judge?

BRACK: I believe she can.

(HEDDA *has a sudden realization.*)

HEDDA: George! —Give me the letter.

GEORGE: Whatever for?

HEDDA: I'll post it. You two friends catch up.

GEORGE: Now Hedda, you know I walk more quickly than you, and it's almost time for the postman to arrive at the mail receptacle.

HEDDA: Maybe...maybe you shouldn't mail it. At all.

GEORGE: Why, Hedda. Of course I should. Especially since it was your idea.

BRACK: This letter sounds significant. Who is the recipient?

HEDDA: No one. Santa Claus.

BRACK: I see. Have you been naughty or nice?

HEDDA: None of your business. *(She turns to* GEORGE.*)* George, please. That letter was Thea's idea, not mine. I don't want him here.

GEORGE: Nonsense. We should do our civic duty to a stranger in town. I'll be back in a minute.

BRACK: Take your time.

*(*GEORGE *exits.)*

BRACK: Now, Mrs Tesman. Where were we?

*(*BRACK *moves to embrace* HEDDA. *She pushes him away.)*

HEDDA: Not now, lover boy. I gotta think.

BRACK: Who is this person that seems to have distracted you?

HEDDA: Good idea. I'll tell you about it, and maybe you can head him off at the pass. He's a degenerate. Someone who has led a decent woman away from her husband. Into a scandalous, immoral relationship that will bring ruin to her innocent reputation.

BRACK: Ah. You're speaking of Eilert Lovborg.

HEDDA: You've heard of him?

BRACK: Naturally. I keep my ear pretty close to the ground, as they say, Mrs Tesman.

HEDDA: So you'll have him arrested?

BRACK: On what charge? He's broken no laws. Except a few natural ones, perhaps. And that was long ago.

HEDDA: Isn't that enough? Whatever happened to the good old-fashioned practice of running people out of town?

BRACK: This is Norway, not the Wild West. We're much more civilized than that.

(Pause)

(BRACK *tries to grab* HEDDA*'s breasts. She pulls away.)*

HEDDA: Get away from me. Who do you think you are?

BRACK: I don't understand this sudden change in attitude, I must say. Perhaps I should go.

HEDDA: No! I'm just...playing with you. You know how I love to play with you. Don't you like playing with me?

BRACK: You have many strange games, Mrs Tesman, and I don't recognize this one.

HEDDA: It's new. The rules are flexible. Just like me.

BRACK: All right. I suppose.

HEDDA: Now let's talk about arresting Eilert Lovborg.

BRACK: Why?

HEDDA: Oh, no reason. Small talk. Think of it as foreplay.

BRACK: I wonder. Didn't you use to have some sort of relationship with this Lovborg fellow? Before you were married?

HEDDA: Good God. Is there nothing else to talk about in this godforsaken town?

BRACK: Well there's the glaciers. But only when things get slow. *(He chuckles to himself.)*

HEDDA: You think that's funny? Do you have the slightest idea how all of this will end? I'm going to kill myself. And you'll be the main cause of it. So laugh it up.

BRACK: This is exceedingly morbid talk.

HEDDA: I told you, new rules. What do I have to do in order to for you to get rid of Eilert Lovborg?

BRACK: Well, let me think. Here's an idea. *(He unzips his pants.)*

(GEORGE enters, a second after.)

GEORGE: Judge Brack? Umm…

BRACK: Ah, Tesman. Where are your nearest facilities? I seem to be in immediate need.

GEORGE: Apparently so. Down the hall to the right. I hope you make it in time.

BRACK: Not to worry. *(He exits.)*

GEORGE: Poor fellow.

(HEDDA sits on the couch and pats it.)

HEDDA: George, please sit down with me for a moment.

GEORGE: Gladly, my love. *(He does so.)* What troubles you?

HEDDA: I don't want you to leave me alone with Brack. Or Eilert Lovborg, when he comes.

GEORGE: We can't even be sure that he—

HEDDA: Oh, he's coming, believe me. He wouldn't miss it for the world. Come to think of it, I don't want you to leave me alone with Thea, Aunt Julie, or even Bertha if she has the bad sense to return here for such a small part.

GEORGE: Why in the world—

HEDDA: Just listen to me. Bad things happen when you're not here.

GEORGE: Why would that be the case?

HEDDA: Because I *make* them happen. I don't even know why. It's my nature, and I keep trying to circumvent it. But it would be so much easier to stop myself if you're in the room. I don't give you enough credit for that. You're not the most exciting guy in the world, but you're a stabilizing presence. And that's what I need right now. Stability—and dependability. Can I depend on you?

GEORGE: Well, naturally, Hedda. I must say, I'm very touched by this sudden tenderness. You certainly have had some unpredictable moods today.

HEDDA: I know. I'm probably bipolar. Which is why I need you here. By my side. I'm too unpredictable for my own good. Do you promise not to leave my side? For anything?

GEORGE: Why, of course, Hedda.

(HEDDA *takes* GEORGE's *hand.*)

HEDDA: I've come to realize that I haven't shown you the proper amount of affection, George. That will change, too. You're my bulwark.

GEORGE: Bulwark? A very interesting word. It has a fascinating etymology from the Middle Dutch. There's "bole", meaning plank, combined with "work", meaning, well, "work". So it's basically a plank, or series of planks, creating a wall. Thus the word describes a defensive fortification. But there's a second theory on its origin—

(HEDDA *kisses* GEORGE *with passion.*)

GEORGE: ...which I forget.

HEDDA: You promise, then? Don't leave me alone—not even for a second.

GEORGE: I promise. I will be glued to you for eternity. Nothing can possibly pry me away.

(BRACK *enters.*)

BRACK: I say, Tesman. You seem to be out of buttermilk.

(GEORGE *jumps up.*)

GEORGE: Of course. I'll go to the corner shop right away.

BRACK: Perhaps some cigars as well?

GEORGE: Capital idea. There's a tobacco shop no more than ten blocks from here. I'll be right back.

(GEORGE *exits, not noticing* HEDDA'*s pleading look.*)

(*Pause.* BRACK *grins at* HEDDA *as he sits next to her, taking* GEORGE'*s place.*)

HEDDA: Shit.

BRACK: Hedda! It's so unlike you to indulge in casual profanity. (*Short pause*) I like it.

(BRACK *tries to kiss* HEDDA, *but she pushes him away.*)

HEDDA: God, I've created a monster. Let's set some ground rules, Casanova.

BRACK: More rules?

HEDDA: Better believe it. (*She produces a legal pad and pen, which she hands to* BRACK.) Here, I'll dictate.

BRACK: What's this for?

HEDDA: A written contract. You're a judge, so I would imagine you're familiar with the concept.

BRACK: For God's sake.

HEDDA: We haven't even started, and you have objections. Perhaps we're both wasting our time.

BRACK: I'm sorry. You may commence.

HEDDA: First of all, I'm a married woman. So anything south of the equator is strictly off limits.

BRACK: Really?

HEDDA: I believe this is a notable advancement over your usual menu of furtive glances and lascivious puns.

BRACK: All right. Agreed.

HEDDA: Second, there will be absolutely no exchange of fluids of any kind.

BRACK: Do I have any input on these rules?

HEDDA: No. Thirdly, all tongues should remain firmly fixed to the roof of the mouth. And not each other's.

BRACK: This hardly seems worth the effort.

HEDDA: Oh, it will be worth it, I assure you. Now write down your side of the bargain.

BRACK: Which is what?

HEDDA: That you will arrange for Lovborg's arrest and imprisonment before the day ends.

BRACK: What? I never agreed to that!

HEDDA: I'm aware of that, silly. That's why we have the *contract*.

BRACK: Hedda, please. Let me provide you with a rudimentary understanding of how the law works. You can't arrest people just because you don't like them.

HEDDA: I won't be arresting anyone. That's your job.

BRACK: No, it isn't. That's the police. They come to me for a warrant, if they find probable cause.

HEDDA: So we're skipping the middleman. You can decide that he's probably guilty, and issue the warrant.

BRACK: Guilty of what?

HEDDA: You can decide that too.

BRACK: How can you be so naïve? First there needs to be some sort of crime. Then you need to establish means, motive and opportunity. And his behavior has been completely above board in all the time he's been here.

HEDDA: See? That's suspicious!

BRACK: Being law-abiding isn't suspicious!

HEDDA: Now who's being naïve?

(BRACK *throws down the pad.*)

BRACK: This is ridiculous! I won't indulge any more talk about arresting Eilert Lovborg.

HEDDA: Fine.

BRACK: Good.

HEDDA: Certainly.

BRACK: Thank heavens! Now where were we?

(BRACK *tries to take* HEDDA's *hand, but she pulls it away.*)

HEDDA: What are you doing?

BRACK: I thought—

HEDDA: I can see what you thought. Sorry, pal. The candy store is closed. (*She moves to the end of the couch.*)

(*Pause.* BRACK *is in torment.*)

BRACK: I suppose…

HEDDA: Yes?

BRACK: I could drum up some reason to bring him in for questioning.

HEDDA: Keep going.

BRACK: Maybe he fits the description of…somebody… who did…something.

HEDDA: Sounds likely.

BRACK: Would that satisfy you?

HEDDA: For the moment. *(She moves closer to him.)* You may now hold my hand. Until I decide to withdraw it.

BRACK: Gee. Thanks.

HEDDA: You're welcome. See how much nicer this is? This is how things should work. You pay me a trifling favor, and your kindness is returned. An agreeable bargain.

BRACK: I suppose.

HEDDA: Now add the part about arresting Eilert Lovborg. And sign it.

BRACK: Mrs Tesman, be reasonable. Such a document could jeopardize my entire career. I can't put that in writing.

HEDDA: I need your guarantee, Judge Brack. What do you suggest?

BRACK: Why don't we…seal it with a kiss?

(BRACK throws himself on HEDDA, stopping her mouth with a kiss as she tries to object.)

(GEORGE enters, carrying a bottle of buttermilk.)

GEORGE: What's this?

(BRACK quickly extricates himself.)

BRACK: Tesman! I was…clearly I was…there's a very simple…

HEDDA: I had something in my eye, and I asked the Judge to see if he could locate it.

BRACK: Yes, I was locating it.

GEORGE: Let me take a look. *(He puts down the bottle and goes to* HEDDA, *opening her eye.)* I don't see anything... though it is slightly bloodshot, I suppose.

HEDDA: I suppose we managed to jar it loose. Probably no more than a speck of dirt.

GEORGE: Well, what does the Bible say? If there's a mote in your eye, get someone or other to pluck it out.

HEDDA: That's not how it—

GEORGE: "Mote" is an odd word, don't you think? Comes from the Greek—

BRACK: You're back a bit sooner than we expected, Tesman.

GEORGE: Yes. I remembered that I have plenty of cigars in the house. Would you like one?

HEDDA: Please no, George. The very idea of it turns my stomach.

GEORGE: Of course, my delicate flower. But I did remember the buttermilk. Would you like me to pour you a glass, Judge?

BRACK: For God's sake, whatever for? I can't stand the sight of—

HEDDA: You did request it, you know. George went to all the trouble...

(BRACK *realizes.*)

BRACK: Ah yes, buttermilk! I thought you said butterscotch. But buttermilk—that hits the spot.

GEORGE: Coming up. *(He exits.)*

BRACK: Good Lord, Hedda. I have forgotten myself. Can you forgive me?

HEDDA: I hope you have not forgotten your promise to me as well.

BRACK: Promise?

HEDDA: Regarding Eilert Lovborg.

GEORGE: *(Offstage)* Lovborg?

(GEORGE enters with buttermilk in a glass, which he hands to BRACK.)

BRACK: Thank you, Tesman. It's very yellow, isn't it? *(He takes a sip, making a face of disgust as he does.)*

GEORGE: You were speaking of Eilert Lovborg, I believe.

BRACK: Yes, we were.

GEORGE: An old friend of mine. I hear he's in town.

BRACK: *(Glancing at HEDDA)* Oh, who told you that?

GEORGE: Mrs Elvsted, actually.

BRACK: Elvsted? Is she the person married to that rural sheriff?

GEORGE: The very one. You may have seen her in passing as you came to the house.

BRACK: Oh, yes, the lovely woman running and holding her head as though her hair were on fire.

GEORGE: Really? How odd. Anyway, she gave us that news this morning. Apparently Lovborg tutored her children near the college.

BRACK: I see. That might explain her presence in town as well. *(He looks at HEDDA again.)* I'm beginning to put some pieces of this puzzle together.

GEORGE: Don't know if there's anything so puzzling about it. I'm told he has published a new book.

BRACK: Yes he has. It has created quite a sensation in the time you've been gone.

GEORGE: Well, good for him.

BRACK: I hesitate to say this, but you may have cause to worry about his return in ways you don't yet realize.

GEORGE: Pardon me?

HEDDA: He's saying that he may compete for your job at the University.

GEORGE: What? With his reputation?

BRACK: I'm afraid Mrs Tesman has—surprisingly—expressed the situation with accuracy. Old failings can be easily replaced by newer triumphs. It appears that you are both being considered for the professorship.

GEORGE: I'm doomed.

BRACK: Not necessarily.

GEORGE: Oh? There's hope?

BRACK: There's talk of a formal competition.

GEORGE: Competition? Between him and me?

BRACK: To determine your academic qualifications.

GEORGE: I'm doomed.

HEDDA: It's not important, George.

GEORGE: If only that were true, Hedda. Do you know how much debt I owe after that five month trip?

HEDDA: You think I married you only to spend my honeymoon in *hostels*? People come in at three A M, spill their change on the floor and wash their underwear in the sink. When they're not stealing yours.

BRACK: Yes, no doubt Mrs Tesman requires the finest hotels, clothes, furnishings—the finest of everything.

HEDDA: You knew my habits when you married me, George.

GEORGE: You're right, of course, both of you. But I was counting on that position at the university. I thought that would solve everything.

HEDDA: I told you not to mail that letter.

GEORGE: My God. I forgot about the letter. I invited Lovborg here tonight.

BRACK: Tonight? But I invited you to my stag party for tonight. Don't you remember?

GEORGE: Stag party?

HEDDA: He doesn't remember. He never remembers.

BRACK: It was in your honor, you know. I wasn't able to throw you a proper bachelor party before you left town.

GEORGE: Oh my. It would be rude of me to forego your invitation, wouldn't it?

BRACK: No matter. I'm sure Lovborg will realize the awkwardness of coming to this household under these circumstances.

(HEDDA groans loudly.)

GEORGE: What's wrong, Hedda?

HEDDA: You two, going through this circular exercise in obliviousness. Over and over. It's like trying to talk sense to Kellyanne Conway. Of course Eilert will come, and of course it will result in disaster.

BRACK: Is that so? And what gives you such gifts of foresight?

HEDDA: Me? What about you? Both of you? Why can't your characters ever learn one damn thing? Why am I the only one around here who doesn't suffer from chronic amnesia? Why is it always up to me?

GEORGE: You must forgive Hedda, Judge. As I said, she's not quite herself today.

BRACK: Yes, I saw some evidence of that while you were gone.

HEDDA: Oh, up yours, you slimy old pervert.

BRACK: I suggest you put Hedda to bed, Tesman. She's downright delirious. I'll come back for you this evening.

GEORGE: By all means, Judge Brack. I look forward to it.

(BRACK *leaves the room.*)

GEORGE: Perhaps we need to think about adjusting our belts a bit, Hedda.

HEDDA: Oh, here it comes.

GEORGE: We may find ourselves living above our means.

HEDDA: No way. I'm not going to take in college students or move to some condominium where I have to attend H O A meetings. Do you hear me, George? I won't have that.

GEORGE: Then maybe reconsider a few of the things you were planning on. Such as your new saddle horse.

HEDDA: Screw the horse, George. I want you to develop a backbone, and not crap in your pants at the slightest sign of competition. You're just as worthy as Eilert Lovborg.

GEORGE: Do you really think so?

HEDDA: Of course not, you idiot. I'm trying to buck you up.

GEORGE: Very kind of you.

HEDDA: Don't make me bored, George. You know what I do when I get bored.

GEORGE: Well, I believe you lie in the bathtub and you—

HEDDA: Besides that. I amuse myself with my father's pistols.

GEORGE: No, not those pistols!

HEDDA: Yes, General Gabler's pistols. They feel warm and firm in my hands.

GEORGE: They frighten me, Hedda. Please don't play with those pistols.

HEDDA: We shall see, George. We shall see! (*She leaves, laughing maniacally.*)

(GEORGE *calls after* HEDDA.)

GEORGE: For God's sake, Hedda! Don't touch those dangerous things! I beg you!

(HEDDA *quickly returns.*)

HEDDA: It's okay, George. I'm just fucking with you.

(*Blackout*)

Scene Two

(*Lights up on* HEDDA, *facing* EILERT LOVBORG, *who has just entered the room, holding a letter.*)

(*He looks around, confused.*)

EILERT: Have I come at a bad time? This feels rather… abrupt.

HEDDA: I skipped ahead. Have a seat, Eilert.

EILERT: Your husband invited me here. I have his letter.

HEDDA: Yes, I tried to prevent that. Without success.

EILERT: This isn't the way I expected to find you—

HEDDA: I know. The sequence is temporarily off, but I expect things will align themselves very shortly. That's why I need to tell you a few things before we're interrupted.

EILERT: Perhaps I should return at another time.

HEDDA: You could work on your listening skills, you know. I'm trying to talk to you about something important.

EILERT: All right, Mrs Tesman.

HEDDA: Oh, jeez, are you going to pretend we don't have a history now? There's no time for that!

EILERT: I don't want to presume...

HEDDA: Presume. For God's sake, presume.

EILERT: All right. I will. I suppose this is easy for you, isn't it? Just like old times. The proud, disdainful, beautiful daughter of the famous General Gabler—still toying with the affections of the man who was once willing to toss all of his own ambitions into the river just for the chance to be close to her. Do you know how hard it is for me to come here after all this time, and once again stare into your cold, piercing eyes? Do you know how much courage it takes for me to just sit here next to you? How much restraint?

HEDDA: See, this is why it didn't work out between us. You're a little intense.

EILERT: You're the one who threatened to shoot me.

HEDDA: Oh come on. Don't exaggerate.

EILERT: I'm the one who found myself staring down the barrel of one your father's damned pistols. Without the slightest doubt that you would pull the trigger, and that I would feel the impact in my heart. Bang!

(BRACK *is heard offstage, responding to the noise.*)

BRACK: *(Offstage)* No, Mrs Tesman! Please don't shoot me!

HEDDA: Now see what you've done. He thinks it's his cue.

EILERT: Cue? What is this? Have you taken another lover?

HEDDA: It's just Judge Brack. *(She yells offstage.)* It's not time yet, Brack! Come back in an hour!

BRACK: *(Offstage)* Don't aim that thing at me!

HEDDA: I'm not aiming anything, you moron! Get lost! *(She turns to* EILERT.*)* Eilert, in the interest of time, I beg you. Don't go to their damn party. Don't have anything to drink. And don't touch anyone's gun, no matter who gives it to you.

EILERT: What is this, some sort of game? If so, I don't find it very amusing.

*(*BRACK *enters from the back.)*

BRACK: Nor do I, Mrs Tesman. You could hurt someone with the way you indiscriminately shoot from your garden door.

HEDDA: I wasn't shooting anything, Brack.

BRACK: This is strange. I see you have company.

HEDDA: Yes. Can we leave it at that?

*(*EILERT *stands and holds out his hand.)*

EILERT: Eilert Lovborg.

BRACK: So I guessed. There's been a lot of discussion about you around here today.

EILERT: Really? I can't imagine why.

HEDDA: Because you're the inciting incident. Though it took you long enough to actually show up. *(Turning to the audience)* Am I right?

BRACK: I believe there was a Mrs Elvsted here today.

EILERT: Thea? Here?

BRACK: I didn't talk to her myself. But I understand she seemed very concerned about your whereabouts.

(EILERT *turns to* HEDDA.)

EILERT: You didn't tell me Thea was here.

HEDDA: What, in the ten seconds before this guy stumbled in? Well, excuse me.

BRACK: Perhaps her husband sent her here to look for you.

EILERT: Not very likely.

BRACK: Ah. I believe I see the situation.

HEDDA: We all see the situation, Brack. With binoculars.

EILERT: Poor Thea. The sacrifices she would make for me. If I were to allow it.

HEDDA: Listen to me, Eilert. Allow it. She's the one for you. The two of you need to find each other as soon as possible and hightail it out of here. That would solve everything. For all concerned.

BRACK: Mrs Tesman! How scandalous! You're speaking about a married woman!

HEDDA: You think I don't know that? Besides, who are you to talk, when you've been playing footsie with me under the dining table for months?

BRACK: Well I never!

HEDDA: And who even talks like that? Besides Margaret Dumont?

EILERT: Mrs Elvsted has been an important companion to me, and helped me through many crises of the soul and spirit. She also did all the research on my new book, at the price of her husband's suspicions about our relationship. In short…I owe my life to her.

HEDDA: She's in love with you.

EILERT: Quite probably. If only she weren't so stupid.

HEDDA: You're one hell of a catch all right.

EILERT: Perhaps that seemed a little harsh.

HEDDA: Just a bit. Who the fuck do you think you are? To call any woman *stupid*?

BRACK: I think he chose the word he meant, Mrs Tesman. Perhaps in comparison to yourself.

HEDDA: I'm aware of that, Brack. He says it in nearly every translation.

EILERT: You seem a little strange, Mrs Tesman. I believe you've changed.

BRACK: She certainly has. Her behavior today has been quite worrisome.

(GEORGE *enters, carrying another stack of books that distracts his vision.*)

GEORGE: What's this? Is my poor Hedda still under the weather?

HEDDA: You have company, George.

(GEORGE *continues to carry the books across the room.*)

GEORGE: Yes, Judge Brack, of course. Let me just discard these books…

EILERT: Hello, Mr Tesman.

(*Startled*, GEORGE *drops the books.*)

GEORGE: My heavens!

HEDDA: Oh, George. Not more books?

GEORGE: My dear fellow—you're here already?

BRACK: He even preceded my arrival, Tesman. How unusual, wouldn't you say? I imagine that your wife was…very accommodating.

HEDDA: You imagine all right.

(GEORGE *moves to* EILERT, *and they shake hands.*)

GEORGE: My dear old friend! How wonderful to see you again.

EILERT: Thank you for your generous invitation, Mr Tesman.

GEORGE: Please, call me George, and I will call you Eilert.

EILERT: Just like the old days, eh?

GEORGE: Yes, please. Speaking of times gone by, I believe you once met my wife.

EILERT: Yes, I knew her well.

HEDDA: Not that well.

EILERT: Quite well.

HEDDA: Somewhat well.

EILERT: Pretty well.

HEDDA: Well enough, I suppose.

GEORGE: Yes…well…I just bought your book, Eilert. It's over here somewhere.

(GEORGE *goes to the stack of books on the floor, and sorts through them.* HEDDA *helps him.*)

EILERT: I see you're still a voracious reader, Tesman.

GEORGE: Oh, yes, though my tastes are a bit academic, I suppose.

HEDDA: There it is.

GEORGE: Where?

HEDDA: The one with the Oprah sticker.

GEORGE: Ah yes. *(He picks up the book.)*

BRACK: They say your sales have been quite impressive.

GEORGE: Indeed? I'm anxious to read it myself.

EILERT: Don't bother. There's not much in it.

GEORGE: Is that so? Doesn't seem that short. Large print, then?

EILERT: I mean the content is insignificant. My new book is much more effective.

GEORGE: New book, you say?

(EILERT produces a packet of paper from his coat pocket.)

EILERT: Yes, I brought it with me. I thought perhaps I could read a bit of it to you. It goes far beyond the constraints of that book.

BRACK: How so?

EILERT: It deals with the future.

GEORGE: The future! Imagine that, Hedda!

HEDDA: Does it say how this play will end?

(They look at her, mystified.)

EILERT: It's simple, really, a continuation of the first book. Except that it goes on to solve all the world's problems.

GEORGE: That does sound like a bestseller, I must say.

EILERT: Yes, I lay out comprehensive but affordable methods to eliminate crime, poverty, war, corruption, disease and environmental pollution. It pretty much makes everything much, much better. Oh yes, and racism. Can't forget racism. Gone. Like that. *(He snaps his fingers.)*

HEDDA: What about sexism?

EILERT: Hmm. Can't say I'm familiar with that term.

HEDDA: Didn't think so.

GEORGE: I'm happy for you, Eilert. Truly, I am.

EILERT: Thank you.

GEORGE: Despite my compulsion to strangle you. Couldn't be happier for you.

EILERT: You're very kind. I'll begin with the Prologue... *(He begins to unwrap the parcel.)*

GEORGE: Oh dear. I'm terribly sorry, Eilert, but I've promised Judge Brack that I'd attend his soiree this evening.

BRACK: Why don't you come with us, Mr Lovborg? The event is in Tesman's honor. Newly married, and all that.

(EILERT looks at HEDDA.)

EILERT: So I've heard.

GEORGE: Yes, do come along, old man.

EILERT: Tempting. But I think it would be best if I declined your invitation, Judge. I don't always do well in those situations.

BRACK: What a shame. Things could get pretty uninhibited.

EILERT: My fear, exactly.

HEDDA: Uninhibited? What a laugh. You won't be missing a thing, Eilert. The most excitement is when they pass around the stereoscope.

BRACK: Hardly.

EILERT: Even so, I assume you will be serving spirits.

GEORGE: What, ghosts?

BRACK: He means liquor, Tesman.

EILERT: I do indeed. I'm afraid those days are behind me.

GEORGE: On second thought, perhaps it would be better for you to stay here, Eilert.

HEDDA: Here? Who said anything about here? He should go back to his hotel. We'll *all* be safer that way.

GEORGE: But I just remembered that Mrs Elvsted plans to be here tonight. She was hoping to see you.

HEDDA: That was more of a maybe.

GEORGE: No, I remember. She made quite a strong point of it.

EILERT: Then I probably should stay here. For Thea's sake.

HEDDA: George, I wonder if you could send a message to Aunt Julie to come over tonight. I do miss her so. And I want to apologize about that stupid bonnet.

GEORGE: I forgot to mention that Aunt Rina has taken a turn for the worse. She's not able to leave her side tonight.

HEDDA: Oh, for God's sake, can't she just put a pillow over her sister's face and come over for an hour or two?

GEORGE: You're not being very considerate, Hedda.

EILERT: It's fine, Tesman. Hedda and I will catch up until Thea arrives. You two go ahead.

HEDDA: Tell you what. Let's go out, Eilert. Someplace public. How about ice skating?

EILERT: We still have to wait for Thea first.

HEDDA: No we don't. She's used to being left behind. You've been doing it to her for months.

EILERT: Which is the reason we should stay.

HEDDA: Since when are you so noble? You weren't that way when…

GEORGE: When what, Hedda?

HEDDA: When he arrived. He made a pass at me, George. I'm highly offended. I won't be alone with him.

(Everyone stares at HEDDA, very concerned. Then they burst out laughing.)

HEDDA: What? Is that so hard to believe?

GEORGE: What a jokester you are today, Hedda!

BRACK: I believe she's acquired a rather German sense of humor.

EILERT: I certainly know better than attempt to make love to Hedda Gabler.

BRACK: As do I.

GEORGE: And I.

(They all look at GEORGE quizzically.)

GEORGE: Changing the subject, old man, I hear rumors that the University intends to put you and I together into the gladiator's ring. To fight it out.

EILERT: That won't be happening, George. You can rest assured.

GEORGE: What do you mean?

EILERT: I have no interest in an academic position. Those are reserved exclusively for timid, minimally talented pedants who are terrified of living a meaningful life.

GEORGE: So the job is mine?

EILERT: If you're able to sacrifice your dignity to that extent. Yes.

GEORGE: You hear that, Hedda? The job is mine!

HEDDA: Congratulations.

BRACK: Yes, good show, Tesman. You showed them, didn't you?

GEORGE: I suppose I did.

HEDDA: I think Eilert helped a little.

GEORGE: Quite right. My deepest gratitude, dear fellow.

EILERT: Whatever.

BRACK: We really should be moving along now, Tesman.

GEORGE: No, I feel like celebrating. How about some punch?

HEDDA: There is no punch, George.

GEORGE: Of course there is. It's in the next room.

HEDDA: Berta wasn't here to put out the punch bowl. And I certainly wasn't going to do it.

GEORGE: But I just saw it.

HEDDA: That's not possible.

GEORGE: I promise you it's there. Would you like some, Judge?

BRACK: I'd love some.

GEORGE: And you, Eilert?

EILERT: No thank you.

GEORGE: You're sure?

HEDDA: He can't indulge, George. Remember?

GEORGE: Hmm? Oh, yes! I completely forgot you were a drunk.

EILERT: I appreciate your sensitivity.

GEORGE: Well, I'll not tempt you further. Come on, Judge.

(The men exit to the next room.)

(HEDDA *calls after them.*)

HEDDA: There's nothing there! You're wasting your exit! *(She turns to* EILERT.*)* All right. Let's get a few things straight. We're not going to talk any more about our previous relationship. What's past is past.

EILERT: Why?

HEDDA: See, that's the kind of question I'd like to avoid. It will just rile you up. There was never anything to it. Ships passing in the night.

EILERT: Except one ship nearly blew a hole in the other ship.

HEDDA: Oh, for God's sake, you act like I'm the only person who threatened to kill you.

EILERT: You are.

HEDDA: Oh. Well, all the more reason to be with Thea. She's not psychotic.

EILERT: You weren't being psychotic. You were in love.

HEDDA: You think there's a difference?

EILERT: All the times we spent—

HEDDA: I don't wanna hear about that. I've forgotten.

EILERT: That's not possible.

HEDDA: Forgotten it all. What we did in bed, what we did next to the bed, what we did in the mattress store. Ancient history. I'm a married woman now.

EILERT: Yes, that's the biggest insult of all. That you would choose George Tesman over me. That—that—pusillanimous pedagogue.

HEDDA: Stop it. You know how alliteration turns me on. But he is my husband, like it or not.

EILERT: I don't like it. And neither do you. You used to be full of life—spontaneity—

HEDDA: Gin.

EILERT: Nonetheless. The very notion that Hedda
Gabler would allow herself to be tied down in such a
stultifying existence…it makes my blood boil.

HEDDA: Oh, stop boiling. Look, you were hot stuff, no
question. The six-pack abs, the motorcycle, the tattoos,
the Clash albums. What girl could resist? Not to
mention the volcanic sex. Remember when the plaster
fell?

EILERT: Of course I do.

HEDDA: Well, I don't! I don't remember any of it,
just like I don't remember the scratches on your back
from the time I got a little too excited. I don't have the
slightest memory. Of any of it. You're like a bad dream
I had a very long time ago. Even if I wanted to, as hard
as I tried, I wouldn't be able to dredge up the slightest
hint of how I used to feel about you. So forget it. And
forget me.

EILERT: I suppose you're right. It's all in the past. It's
over.

HEDDA: Damn right.

(Pause)

*(*HEDDA *violently pulls* EILERT *to her and clamps her mouth
over his.)*

*(*GEORGE *enters behind* EILERT, *carrying two glasses of
punch.)*

GEORGE: Hedda!

EILERT: Oh my God. Tesman.

GEORGE: What is in your eyes now? Maybe you need
new mascara. Excuse me, Eilert. My turn to take a look.

*(*EILERT *moves away rapidly while* GEORGE *pulls her eyes
open.)*

GEORGE: Nothing. I suppose you got it first, Eilert. My thanks to you.

EILERT: You're...welcome?

GEORGE: Anyway, I thought Hedda would like some punch.

HEDDA: You mean there *was* punch? I'm gonna *kill* that stage manager.

EILERT: George, I thought I made it clear...

GEORGE: I know, I know. The second glass is for Mrs Elvsted. When she arrives.

HEDDA: She won't want any. And neither do I.

GEORGE: It's very fizzy.

HEDDA: No, George.

GEORGE: All right, all right. I'll just put them down here.

HEDDA: No, no, take them away! I don't want any punch in this room!

(BRACK *enters, with an enormous goblet full of punch.*)

BRACK: We should be on our way, Tesman. Sure you won't join us, Mr Lovborg?

EILERT: Quite certain.

BRACK: All right. It's your funeral.

HEDDA: Why did you put it that way?

BRACK: No reason. (*He sets down the enormous goblet.*) We better go.

HEDDA: Stay here. It's not that far to the green room.

GEORGE: Honestly, Hedda. Who would paint a room green? And why?

(BRACK *and* GEORGE *exit.*)

(HEDDA *stands and moves toward the punch glasses.*)

HEDDA: Let me get rid of these glasses.

EILERT: Not now. We need to talk about what just happened here.

(EILERT *grabs* HEDDA *by the arm.*)

HEDDA: I really need to deal with this punch, Eilert. Before we're interrupted.

(GEORGE *bursts in, pulling* THEA *behind him.* EILERT *releases* HEDDA.)

GEORGE: Look who's here! Mrs Elvsted!

HEDDA: *Damn* it, George. She's not due yet!

GEORGE: Well, it's very confusing to me without Berta. Was I supposed to let her stand out on the front porch? That just didn't seem right.

HEDDA: You might as well come in, Thea. I believe you two know each other.

EILERT: Mrs Elvsted.

THEA: Mr Lovborg.

HEDDA: Oh God. This is going to be a long night.

(BRACK *enters.*)

BRACK: Are we done here, Tesman?

GEORGE: Yes, by all means, let's go.

(BRACK *hands* EILERT *a card.*)

BRACK: Here's my address, if you find yourself craving a bit more…entertainment.

GEORGE: Hedda can be very entertaining.

BRACK: So I've discovered.

HEDDA: Subtle.

GEORGE: Goodbye, all. Don't do anything I wouldn't do.

HEDDA: That doesn't leave us with much, George.

(GEORGE *exits, followed by a slow moving* BRACK, *who walks backwards.*)

BRACK: Have...fun. As I know you will.

HEDDA: We all know you're the bad guy, Brack. Quit acting like you're in some 19th century melodrama. Even if you are.

(BRACK *takes a sinister bow, turns and exits.*)

HEDDA: Thank God they're gone. Now we can sort things out properly. Thea, go sit next to Eilert.

THEA: Really? I would have thought you'd want to sit there.

HEDDA: Nonsense. This is a reunion, isn't it? Go sit on his lap if you want to.

THEA: I think this is sufficient. (*She sits a respectable distance from* EILERT *on the couch.*)

HEDDA: Good. Now let me get rid of these punch glasses. (*She picks them up.*)

THEA: Punch! Oh, I would love some.

HEDDA: Sure, help yourself.

(HEDDA *hands* THEA *a glass.*)

(HEDDA *starts offstage, but is stopped by* EILERT.)

EILERT: You haven't offered me one.

(*Pause*)

HEDDA: Please, Eilert, you know perfectly well that you can't have this.

EILERT: Who says?

HEDDA: *You* did. About three minutes ago.

EILERT: That was out of politeness. I can certainly manage a little punch. You act like I have no self-control.

HEDDA: Why tempt fate?

EILERT: Oh—so now I can't handle temptation?

HEDDA: That's not what I said.

EILERT: Then who did? Thea?

(THEA *puts her glass down.*)

THEA: I don't think I want any after all.

EILERT: *(To* THEA*)* What have you been telling her behind my back?

THEA: Nothing!

EILERT: It's none of her business!

HEDDA: She didn't have to say anything, Eilert. You've been in the papers.

EILERT: I see. I'm surrounded by hypocrites. Who pretend to respect me, but secretly think I'm an inebriate!

HEDDA: There's no secret! Everybody knows!

EILERT: Very well. *(He takes* HEDDA's *glass, and downs it one gulp. Then he grabs* THEA's *glass, and does the same.)*

HEDDA: This is exactly what I was trying to prevent.

EILERT: You think you can have such control over other people?

HEDDA: No, that's what I *used* to think. But it led to tragedy.

EILERT: Well, don't worry about me. Worry about yourself!

HEDDA: That's what I'm doing!

(EILERT *finishes the remainder of* BRACK's *goblet.*)

THEA: I asked you to protect him, Hedda. Now see what you've done.

HEDDA: Me? I'm doing everything I can to avert this!

EILERT: Wait a minute! *Protect* me? Protect me from what?

THEA: Yourself!

HEDDA: Oh God, Thea, shut up! She didn't mean that!

EILERT: I see what's going on here. The two of you have conspired to keep me under surveillance, in case I stray! Like a pet dog!

HEDDA: Nobody thinks you're a dog, Eilert!

EILERT: Why not? If I'm to be treated like a dog, I might as well act like one! *(He goes to a corner vase and urinates into it.)*

HEDDA: I hope they replace that prop.

THEA: Eilert! I can't bear this! Please come to your senses!

(EILERT zips up and turns to her.)

EILERT: Did you even come here on your own volition? Or did your husband send you to bring me back?

THEA: Of course not! He knows nothing about this!

EILERT: Don't lie to me. I owe him money from our last poker game. I thought he'd have the guts to come for it himself.

THEA: He doesn't even play poker! He has a gambling problem.

EILERT: And I suppose I have a drinking problem.

HEDDA: Everybody knows that! *(She turns to* THEA.*)* And by the way, co-dependency is not that sexy. *(To the audience)* That goes for all of you.

EILERT: I think I'll go to Judge Brack's party after all. Away from the prying eyes of women who think so little of me.

HEDDA: Don't go there, Eilert! Stay with us. We'll play Scrabble. And we'll let you win.

EILERT: You don't think I can win on my own?

HEDDA: That's not what I meant.

EILERT: Goodbye, Mrs Tesman. And Goodbye, Mrs Elvsted. Don't wait up for me.

HEDDA: We won't.

THEA: I will.

HEDDA: Shut up, Thea. Eilert. Give me your manuscript. I can keep it safe.

EILERT: You must be joking. Safe with you? You'd probably burn it.

HEDDA: Wow. You do know me well.

EILERT: The next time you see me, I will have vine leaves in my hair!

HEDDA: Vine leaves? Who the hell said anything about vine leaves? (*To* THEA) Did you mention vine leaves?

THEA: I don't think so.

EILERT: Good night to you both! (*He storms out.*)

THEA: Oh, Hedda! What has happened? What will we do? Where is your bathroom?

HEDDA: Good questions. Be quiet and let me think.

(THEA *stands.*)

THEA: I hope it's this way.

HEDDA: There's always the vase.

(THEA *runs off.* HEDDA *turns to the audience.*)

HEDDA: So. How am I doing? Don't answer that. I know. Crashing and burning. All this fricking effort, and you see the results. Fruitless. Nada. I've reached exactly the same point as always, with exactly the same

results. With no way out. That old Norwegian is one
clever son of a bitch. I might as well blow my brains
out now, and not wait for the… *(She reconsiders.)* Hold
on. I can't give up now. There's plenty more to come,
believe me. All sorts of plot points, with manuscripts,
and gunshots, and attempted blackmail. But as far as
I'm concerned, *nothing* is predetermined, I don't care
who wrote it. Nothing *has* to happen. I'll make sure
it doesn't. I'm pretty smart. I just have to try harder.
A battle of wills. My will against his. It's just you and
me now, Ibsen. You hear me? You won't be taking me
down tonight. Nothing can stop me. *Nothing*—except…
maybe an intermission.

(Blackout)

END OF ACT ONE

ACT TWO

Scene One

(Early morning. The light is dim.)

(THEA is asleep on the couch, while HEDDA stands behind her holding a letter, trying to read it by candlelight.)

(The paper begins to smoke with the beginning of a flame.)

HEDDA: Ow! *(She shakes the paper, accidentally dropping it onto THEA's head.)* Oh no. Thea! Thea, wake up! *(She shakes THEA and tries to pull the smoldering paper from her hair.)*

(THEA stirs.)

THEA: What? What is it?

HEDDA: Your hair.

THEA: My hair? What about it?

HEDDA: It's...

(THEA touches her hair.)

THEA: On fire! My hair is on fire!

HEDDA: Nothing so dramatic. I just dropped a piece of paper—

(THEA dislodges the smoldering paper.)

THEA: On my hair? You put a burning piece of paper on my hair! Admit it.

HEDDA: I just said I did.

THEA: Why are you always trying to burn my hair?

HEDDA: I'm not! It was an accident.

THEA: Leave my hair alone, once and for all!

HEDDA: I will, I promise.

THEA: What time is it?

HEDDA: After seven.

THEA: Where's Eilert? Have you sent him away?

HEDDA: No. He hasn't returned yet.

THEA: A likely story. I'd like to see your husband and see what he says about it.

HEDDA: So would I. But he hasn't come home either.

THEA: What? Where is he?

HEDDA: I don't know. Probably still at Judge Brack's.

THEA: So he could be anywhere.

HEDDA: Yes. Listen to me, Thea. Go back to your husband. A country girl like you doesn't belong in the big city. Especially with your attraction to addicts.

THEA: I suppose you think I'm pretty stupid.

HEDDA: Not me. But Eilert does.

THEA: That's a lie.

HEDDA: I swear. That's what he told me. He's not worth the wait, Thea. Go home.

THEA: You've always been jealous of me.

HEDDA: That's true.

THEA: And my hair!

HEDDA: I told you it was an accident!

(GEORGE *enters, trying to hide his face with his hat and tiptoe out of the room.*)

HEDDA: We've already seen you, George.

GEORGE: Damn it. (*He lowers his hat.*)

HEDDA: I suppose you had a fine old time, coming in this late.

GEORGE: Have you been up all night, Hedda? Waiting for me?

THEA: Not just her.

GEORGE: Ah. Mrs Elvsted. I thought you would have left long ago.

HEDDA: In the middle of the night? Without anyone to escort her? Where do you think we live, Grover's Corners?

THEA: Where is Eilert? Do you know?

GEORGE: I'm not sure. I mean, I saw him at first, of course. We got there early, and Judge Brack had to hang the twinkling lights and blow up the balloons.

HEDDA: Somehow that's not how I pictured this party.

GEORGE: So Eilert sat down with me and began to read from his new manuscript. And what a book it is, Hedda! It's a work of genius. Absolutely stunning in its insight, its style, its originality…

HEDDA: Did you understand it?

GEORGE: Not a word.

THEA: Did he mention me?

GEORGE: Yes, I believe he did. Later on, after the…what do you call it…

HEDDA: Orgy.

GEORGE: He made a long, slurred and mostly incomprehensible speech about the woman that had inspired him to write it. I assume he meant you, Mrs Elvsted.

THEA: I suppose.

HEDDA: Unless he meant—

THEA: He meant me, all right? *I'm* his inspiration. So let's get that straight.

HEDDA: Yes ma'am.

THEA: Where is Eilert now?

GEORGE: I'm afraid I lost track of him at the end of the party.

HEDDA: I'm sure he'll be along any minute, Thea. Why don't you use my bedroom and get some more sleep.

THEA: That's very kind of you.

HEDDA: Just don't touch anything.

THEA: Thank you. *(She exits.)*

GEORGE: Hedda, I'm afraid I have a confession to make. *(He pulls* EILERT'*s manuscript from his jacket.)*

HEDDA: Get that out of here, George! I don't want that in this house!

GEORGE: You don't even know what it is.

HEDDA: It's Eilert's manuscript, isn't it?

GEORGE: Oh. You do know what it is.

HEDDA: He brought it here earlier. Remember?

GEORGE: Well, I didn't want to embarrass poor Mrs Elvsted. She already seems to idolize Lovborg to such an unnatural degree.

HEDDA: Nothing unnatural about it, George. She's in love with him.

GEORGE: Oh. That would explain a few things.

HEDDA: So you were saying you found that on the street.

GEORGE: I never said any such thing.

HEDDA: My apologies. Where did you find it?

GEORGE: On the street. As you somehow guessed. There it was lying on the sidewalk, on my way home from Judge Brack's house. Can you imagine poor Eilert losing something so precious, just because he'd had a little too much to drink? What an unlikely coincidence that I happened to find it.

HEDDA: Coincidence, maybe, bad dramaturgy, certainly. It's all part of the setup for what happens later. It's preordained that you find it and bring it back to our house in order to create catastrophe.

GEORGE: You're talking nonsense. I was very fortunate to find it. And I thank God I did.

HEDDA: I beg you to listen to me, George. Throw that thing away or you'll be sorry.

GEORGE: Absolutely not. Lovborg will be in utter panic when he sobers up and realizes it's gone.

HEDDA: Then take it back where you found it. He'll retrace his steps. Like anyone who loses their car keys. There's even an app for that. He'll find it, I promise you.

GEORGE: Much too risky, Hedda. Any fool could pick it up.

HEDDA: It doesn't take any fool. It only takes one.

GEORGE: Precisely. So thank heavens it was me.

HEDDA: Here's another idea. Give it to Thea. She knows how to find Eilert. And the two of them can call an Uber and get out of our hair for the rest of time. And we'll both be alive and happy. Well, alive at least.

GEORGE: Thea, you say.

HEDDA: Yes, isn't that a reasonable solution? She'll take it right to him.

GEORGE: I guess that does make sense.

HEDDA: Great. Hand it over and I'll wake her up.

GEORGE: Oh, let the poor girl sleep, Hedda. Clearly she's had a rough night.

HEDDA: It was no picnic for me either, George.

GEORGE: Then you should catch up on your own rest, don't you think? I'll just put this here. *(He lays the manuscript down on the writing desk. He sees the envelope there.)* What's this?

(HEDDA turns to the audience.)

HEDDA: The letter! I forgot about that. Damn that Thea and her flammable hair!

GEORGE: Was there a letter for me from Aunt Julie?

(HEDDA panics, looking around the couch for the charred letter.)

HEDDA: What makes you think so?

GEORGE: I recognize her handwriting. But this envelope is empty. Did you read it, Hedda?

HEDDA: I might have.

GEORGE: Where is it now? What did it say?

(HEDDA's on the floor, looking under the couch.)

HEDDA: Oh, you know Aunt Julia. Full of trivial gossip about women who smoke and wear pants. Nothing important. *(Turning to the audience)* You could do more than just sit there, you know. Where'd it go?

(GEORGE finds the letter behind the couch.)

GEORGE: Here it is.

HEDDA: *(To the audience, with disgust)* Thanks a lot. *(She stands up.)* Give it to me, George. It will only upset you.

GEORGE: Oh my heavens! Poor Aunt Rina has taken a turn for the worse.

HEDDA: Of course she has. She's been making the same turn for months now. Ignore it.

GEORGE: She's dying, Hedda.

HEDDA: I don't want to sound insensitive.

GEORGE: That's more like it.

HEDDA: But I really don't care.

GEORGE: Hedda!

HEDDA: You can't leave me tonight, George. Bad things will happen. You promised you'd stay with me no matter what happens.

GEORGE: Well, clearly this is an exception.

HEDDA: No exceptions!

(BRACK *is heard from offstage.*)

BRACK: Tesman! Are you home?

GEORGE: Ah, excellent timing! Here's Judge Brack to occupy you until I return!

HEDDA: Occupy is right. Let me hide this first.

(HEDDA *quickly puts the manuscript into a cabinet or drawer, as* GEORGE *briefly blocks the door.*)

BRACK: There you are.

GEORGE: Good morning, Judge. No time for you to change your clothes either, I suppose.

BRACK: I wanted to make sure you made it home safely. And Lovborg.

GEORGE: I just got here. But I know nothing about Lovborg.

BRACK: I'm sorry to hear that. He seemed to be have lost all control when I last saw him.

GEORGE: Yes, poor fellow.

BRACK: You wouldn't have any idea where he is, Mrs Tesman?

HEDDA: Why me? You think I'm hiding him under the couch?

BRACK: I wouldn't put it past you.

GEORGE: He's not there. We just looked.

BRACK: Well then. Perhaps he'll turn up if we wait.

GEORGE: I'm afraid you'll have to wait without me.

BRACK: Oh?

GEORGE: My Aunt Rina seems to be at death's door.

BRACK: Then by no means should I detain you.

HEDDA: Maybe Judge Brack would be kind enough to accompany you.

BRACK: Oh, I don't think my presence would be welcome at such a deeply personal time.

GEORGE: Yes, it's best that I go alone. *(To* HEDDA*)* You'll remember to wake Mrs Elvsted, won't you, Hedda?

HEDDA: Yes, George.

GEORGE: And give her the…thing?

HEDDA: Yes, George.

GEORGE: So that she can give it to…you know who?

HEDDA: For God's sake, it's not espionage, George. Go to your Aunt.

*(*GEORGE *nods and exits.)*

BRACK: What was all that about?

HEDDA: Nothing. What are you doing here so early, Judge?

BRACK: Looking for Eilert Lovborg. Like everyone else in town. Did I hear Mrs Elvsted is still here?

HEDDA: Yes, sleeping. The poor woman is very worried about him.

BRACK: As well she should be.

HEDDA: Just spill it, Brack.

BRACK: I would like to report this delicately. He went to a house of ill repute.

HEDDA: Your place.

BRACK: After that! He went to a brothel.

HEDDA: And how do you know this?

BRACK: I was...in the general vicinity. Anyway, I'm told he became very upset when he realized he had lost his wallet. And something else, I'm not sure what. He accused the hostess, and they came to blows.

HEDDA: Did this woman have red hair?

BRACK: You astonish me, Mrs Tesman. Are you friends with this person?

HEDDA: Only on Facebook. Is she a singer?

BRACK: She may have been some sort of chanteuse at one time. Now she does other things with her mouth.

HEDDA: Don't be disgusting. Where is Eilert now? Don't tell me. I know that too. Jail.

BRACK: Quite right. The police were called, and Lovborg accosted one of them. He spent the night in a cell, and was released this morning.

HEDDA: Whereas with you, the cops looked the other way.

BRACK: I thought I should warn you of these developments in case Lovborg does return here. After all, you and your husband are respectable citizens. Every decent home should close their doors to him.

HEDDA: But still leave them open to you.

BRACK: Naturally. You should inform Mrs Elvsted, so that she will return to her husband forthwith.

HEDDA: She'll refuse. She's not afraid of scandal.

BRACK: I see. Can you say the same?

HEDDA: Sure. I've got nothing to hide.

BRACK: I wish I could share your indifference. But as I remember, we all began our celebrations…here.

HEDDA: So what?

BRACK: Oh, I suspect Lovborg will drag you into this mess to protect himself. You and your husband. And Mrs Elvsted.

HEDDA: And you.

BRACK: No. Not me. I was never here. I have people who can swear to that.

HEDDA: Who do you think you are? If I go down, you go down with me.

BRACK: Oh my.

HEDDA: Can you get your mind out of the gutter for two seconds? What's it to you if he comes here?

BRACK: Why, I have my own reputation to think of, you know. If I were you, I would give my warnings some serious thought.

HEDDA: You mean threats.

BRACK: I speak to you as a friend. Who am I to threaten you?

HEDDA: That's right, Brack. You have no say over me.

BRACK: None at all. And with luck, nothing will happen.

HEDDA: I'm a lucky girl.

BRACK: Your luck might change.

HEDDA: I think you should leave now. Before you grow a moustache and begin to twirl it.

BRACK: By all means. As a precaution, I'll leave through the garden.

HEDDA: God, I hate you. To think I was dumb enough to grab your ass. A lot of good that did me.

BRACK: Good morning, Mrs Tesman. *(He exits through the back.)*

HEDDA: Okay. Lovborg will be here soon. I gotta act fast. The pistols. I've got to get rid of them. They can't be here when he returns. *(She opens the cupboard and removes a wooden box.)*

(EILERT enters without warning, his hair and clothes stained and in disarray.)

EILERT: So. That went well.

HEDDA: I'll be right with you, Eilert.

EILERT: What's in the box?

HEDDA: Nothing. Just throwing away some stale macaroons. Be right back.

EILERT: What if I'd like one?

HEDDA: I told you, they're stale.

EILERT: I haven't had anything to eat all night.

HEDDA: Believe me, you don't want these. You'll get the runs.

EILERT: Stop playing with me. Those aren't macaroons. You think I don't recognize your father's pistol case?

HEDDA: You're mistaken.

EILERT: His insignia is right there. Etched into the wood. "G G." For General Gabler.

HEDDA: That's the cookie company. G G Cookies, located in the North Hills area of Philadelphia. Google it if you don't believe me! *(To the audience)* You too!

EILERT: You threatened to shoot me. You think I don't remember where you got the gun?

HEDDA: Fine. Have it your way. *(She puts the box down and pulls out one of the pistols. She aims it at him.)* We'll try this a second time.

EILERT: You didn't have the guts the first time. You think you can do it now?

HEDDA: I've got guts galore.

EILERT: You want me dead?

HEDDA: Better you than me.

EILERT: And who wants you dead?

HEDDA: Henrik Ibsen.

EILERT: Who's this? Yet another lover?

HEDDA: If only. He wants you dead too. But I'll kill you first. Thus saving my own life. You're toast either way.

EILERT: Then do it. *(He steps toward her, takes her hand, and places the pistol against his own forehead. He closes his eyes.)* I want you to do it. I have nothing left to live for. I have already taken my own life and discarded it. Like trash. That's how little I think of my life. I've already lost it—I don't even remember where.

HEDDA: Your own life…you're talking about your manuscript!

EILERT: Yes, my book. It's gone forever.

(HEDDA takes her hand away, leaving EILERT still holding the pistol against his forehead, his eyes still closed)

HEDDA: This is so simple! No bloodshed necessary! I'll just give it back to you! Then everything will be fine.

EILERT: What are you talking about?

HEDDA: I have your manuscript!

EILERT: You? (*He opens her eyes, sees that she's moved away, and puts down the pistol.*)

(HEDDA *runs to the cupboard.*)

HEDDA: Yes! In a particularly clumsy plot point, my husband found it out on the street, and gave it to me. Ordinarily I'd just burn it out of perversity, but that turns out to be a really bad decision. If I just give it to you now, then neither of us will have to die! True, it's a pretty shitty ending dramatically, but who cares?

EILERT: Is this possible? You have it in your possession?

HEDDA: Behold! (*She throws open the cupboard. There's nothing there.*) Oh come on! (*She searches the shelves.*) It was just here!

EILERT: Ah, of course. A joke at my expense. To be expected from you, I suppose. And your cruel nature.

HEDDA: Somebody's really messing with me. (*She calls offstage.*) Hey, assholes! Anyone back there? There's a prop missing!

EILERT: You know, Hedda, I'm beginning to worry about you.

HEDDA: Oh cram it, Lovborg. You don't know anything.

(THEA *enters, rubbing her eyes.*)

THEA: What's the commotion? Eilert! You're safe!

(THEA *runs to* EILERT *and throws her arms around him. He pushes her away.*)

EILERT: That's all over now, Mrs Elvsted.

THEA: What's over?

EILERT: Whatever was between us, or whatever we thought was between us. There's no going ahead together.

HEDDA: Oh God. I *hate* this part.

THEA: What are you saying?

EILERT: We have no use for each other now. I'm finished. With my work, with my life, with you.

THEA: Finished? How dare you? After I've devoted my every waking hour to assisting you in your masterpiece?

EILERT: Yes. Did I ever thank you for that?

THEA: It doesn't matter. Everything will change when we publish your new book.

EILERT: There won't be a book, Thea. It's gone.

THEA: Gone? What do you mean?

HEDDA: It's not gone! It's around here somewhere! I'll be right back! (*She runs offstage.*)

EILERT: Listen to me, Thea. I've destroyed it with my own hands.

THEA: Destroyed it!

EILERT: Tore it into a thousand pieces. And scattered them into the sea. To drift away and sink. Just like myself.

(HEDDA *runs back on, dragging the unfortunate* STAGEHAND *from the opening scene.*)

HEDDA: There will be no drifting or sinking while I'm around. Come here, you. Now look! Where's that manuscript? I put it right there!

(*Mystified by her behavior, the* STAGEHAND *looks in the cabinet.*)

HEDDA: Come on, what'd you do with it? This cabinet has a false back, doesn't it? (*She struggles to push the back of the cabinet—it doesn't budge.*)

(*The* STAGEHAND *looks wide-eyed at* EILERT *and* THEA.)

HEDDA: Don't look at them—their characters are completely oblivious. Go off and look for it! Before I complain to Equity.

(*The* STAGEHAND *runs off, terrified.*)

HEDDA: What did I miss?

THEA: Eilert was just telling me how he murdered our child.

HEDDA: Wow. You really go straight for the pathos, don't you?

EILERT: She's right, Hedda. That's what I am. A child murderer. I don't deserve to live.

HEDDA: Don't exaggerate. You're not a psycho. Just more of a low-level pretty boy scumbag.

EILERT: Very true. Who cares about the ruminations of such a person?

THEA: I do, Eilert. They are your thoughts. Which I helped you to compile, arrange, edit, rewrite and footnote. From the incomprehensible mush of your pointless mutterings into shiny, flawless prose. But I take no credit. They're still your thoughts. And as such, dear to me.

EILERT: Well, now they're fish food.

HEDDA: Oh stop that. Neither of you need to be so melodramatic.

THEA: Hedda's right. There's no point in discussing this further.

HEDDA: Thank you.

THEA: I'll just go kill myself. (*She starts to exit.*)

EILERT: I'm right behind you.

HEDDA: Thea! Come back here!

(But THEA*'s gone.)*

HEDDA: You stupid jerk. How could you tell her something like that?

EILERT: I did it for her. To send her back to the thick but dependable arms of her halfwit husband. That's where she belongs.

HEDDA: She belongs with you! Because she loves you— the poor sap.

EILERT: Yes, it's my fate to ruin everything I touch. Maybe you and I could have had a chance.

HEDDA: No. We never had a chance.

EILERT: Maybe under different circumstances.

HEDDA: What circumstances?

EILERT: I'm talking rhetoricially. God. Why does everything have to be so hard? *(He exits.)*

HEDDA: That's that. The last anyone will see of Eilert Lovborg.

*(*EILERT *returns.)*

EILERT: Sorry. Forgot something. *(He heads to the pistol case, and picks one up.)* Mind if I borrow this?

HEDDA: *(Resigned)* Sure, what the hell.

*(*EILERT *exits again.)*

HEDDA: Now he has my father's pistol. So that looks incriminating. And Brack will use that against me. But no one has to know he ever came back here. He could have stolen the gun last night, when everyone was here. Why not? I may have found a plot hole. *(She becomes energized.)*

Sure. Lovborg took it last night, and George found
the manuscript, and he can return it to him as soon
as I find it, no harm done, George exchanges the
manuscript for the pistol, and no one gets hurt, and
Brack has nothing on me, and George gets the job, and
Eilert and Thea go on the lam from her husband and go
on a crime spree for all I care, because I'm alive. *(Pause)*
And married to George. And we have our boring little
life where I give afternoon teas for faculty wives and
long for my freedom. But who needs freedom? I'll have
George, and he'll have me, and he'll have Aunt Julia,
and I'll go find Berta and she'll have us, and I can go
ahead and have this ba— *(She holds her belly, realizing
what she almost said.)* I'll think about that later. Right
now I have to gather up all my old correspondence
with Eilert. And destroy it. No one will point their
fingers at me. *(She calls offstage.)* Hey! You back there!
Come out here!

(The nervous STAGEHAND *comes on again.* HEDDA
whispers in his ear, then pushes him toward the exit.)

*(He looks at her strangely, then worriedly whispers
something in* HEDDA's *ear.)*

HEDDA: Yes, I know what anachronistic means. Now
go find it. Probably one in the box office.

(The STAGEHAND *runs off.)*

*(*HEDDA *goes to the desk and opens a secret compartment.
She pulls out a stack of paper.)*

HEDDA: Here they are. My secret stash. These letters
represent my entire romantic past with Eilert Lovborg.
(She kisses them.)

(The STAGEHAND *reenters, carrying a paper shredder.)*

HEDDA: Put it down there.

(The STAGEHAND *puts it down on a table, then runs off.)*

(HEDDA *turns on the shredder and starts feeding it the stack of paper.*)

HEDDA: Goodbye, Eilert. What matters is now is survival. And survival means stability, and dependability and sameness, and repetition, mind-numbingly constant repetition that wears you down until you're grateful that you can just get out of bed in the morning, even though you secretly pray for the deep dark slumber of eternal rest, but you mustn't think such thoughts, because you have to get up and listen to Aunt Julia prattle on about her dying sister, and George speculate about some obscure battle in ancient who-gives-a-shit, and it takes all the energy you can muster just to pretend to listen, and where is Berta with your order from the pharmacist, how does anyone expect you to get through another day without your demerol? I'm so happy to put all this behind me once and for all. The last page. Thank God. I can't believe I kept this stuff around all these years. (*She reads the final page.*) "Dedicated to Mrs Thea Elvsted, to whom I owe everything. This book would not have been possible without her." Huh. (*Realizing she has destroyed* EILERT's *manuscript.*) NOOOOOOOOOOOOOOOO—

(*Blackout*)

Scene Two

(*Lights up on* HEDDA, *hours later. She is still facing the shredder, mid-scream.* JULIA *is standing behind her at a distance, watching with concern.*)

HEDDA: —OOOOOOOOOOOOOOOO!

(HEDDA *catches her breath, then turns around to see* JULIA, *staring at her.*)

HEDDA: NOOOOOOOOOOOOOOOOO! (*She composes herself again.*) Hi, Aunt Julie. What's up?

JULIA: My heavens, Hedda! What has been happening around here?

HEDDA: Oh, same old same old. And what's new with you?

JULIA: My sister died.

HEDDA: Not exactly news, but I guess it will do.

JULIA: Her final moments were quite peaceful.

HEDDA: Ah. So you weren't there?

JULIA: Of course I was. And George, of course. We said our goodbyes.

HEDDA: Well, I'm sure that encouraged her to move things along.

JULIA: I see your mood is still unpredictable.

HEDDA: Yeah, that's me today. I'm all over the map.

JULIA: And what in the world is that contraption?

HEDDA: Espresso machine. Want some?

JULIA: No thank you. I don't intend to stay very long. I just thought I should be the one to inform you of this sad business. George is still there, handling the final details.

HEDDA: He is frightfully good at details.

JULIA: Yes, he's been quite a comfort to me. He even offered to have me move in with the two of you.

HEDDA: Did he now?

JULIA: Though I'm not quite ready for such a big transition after a lifetime in one place. Maybe in a day or two.

HEDDA: We'll clear out the dungeon.

JULIA: I'm quite used to being a caretaker, you know. So if there are any sudden developments in this household, perhaps I could be of use again. I'd be so happy to watch over any…new additions. You know— the pitter-patter of little feet?

HEDDA: Funny you should say that. Do you like pit bulls? I thought we could use one around here. To scare off the salesmen. Maybe you could take it for walks, sharpen its teeth, stuff like that.

JULIA: I was hoping for some…different news. Perhaps a bundle of joy is on the way?

HEDDA: If you're hoping to score some pot, I think there's a guy down the street. Knock twice and show your ankles.

JULIA: Oh, you're impossible.

HEDDA: Look, I'm in no mood to fight with you today. Come back tomorrow and I won't even be here.

JULIA: Are you planning to take another trip already?

HEDDA: Not my plan, believe me. I don't get any say in the matter.

JULIA: Well, we'll all miss you. When will you return?

HEDDA: In time for the next performance, I imagine.

JULIA: More cryptic talk.

HEDDA: Cryptic! Hey, that's good. Pretty clever, as puns go.

JULIA: Pardon?

HEDDA: Too bad George isn't here. He could tell us the etymology and we could all take a nap.

(GEORGE *enters, exhausted.*)

GEORGE: I could use a nap myself.

HEDDA: Aunt Julie told me the news, or rather, the thing that barely qualifies as news.

GEORGE: Yes, poor Rina.

JULIA: Have you finished with all the final arrangements already?

GEORGE: I'm afraid not. I got stuck on casket linings. Satin, silk, velvet, suede, I'm not used to such decisions. I only own one pair of shoes. Besides, it occurred to me that she's dead.

JULIA: Yes?

GEORGE: So what possible difference would it make to Rina anyway?

JULIA: George! I'm shocked! That sounds like something Hedda would say!

HEDDA: You know, it kinda does.

GEORGE: It's just that…all these horrible developments with Lovborg, and now Rina's dead. It all makes me question whether I'm leading a meaningful life.

JULIA: Well, stop it! At once!

GEORGE: All right. Anything to eat?

HEDDA: George, did you discuss the possibility of Aunt Julie living with us?

GEORGE: I might have mentioned something along those lines.

HEDDA: Without asking me?

GEORGE: Well, what's the point of that, we all know your great affection for Julie. It's obvious to anyone who knows you, that you would make room for her in a second.

JULIA: How sweet of you, Hedda! It warms my heart to hear you say that. Or even to hear George say it for you!

(She hugs HEDDA, *who tolerates it and scowls at* GEORGE.)

(JULIA *disengages herself.)*

JULIA: I'll start bringing over some things tomorrow. I'll start with my grandmother's four poster bed.

GEORGE: I'm sure we can arrange a new bed that will be comfortable for you.

JULIA: Oh I won't sleep in it. Sentimental, I suppose. *(She exits.)*

HEDDA: You don't seem that heartbroken about Aunt Rina.

GEORGE: I'm just worried about Eilert. I ran into Thea on the way here.

(HEDDA *turns to the audience.)*

HEDDA: Which is by no means another coincidence.

GEORGE: Anyway, she told me the most astonishing thing. Is it true that Lovborg turned up here after I left? And he claimed he tore his manuscript to pieces?

HEDDA: That pretty much sums it up.

GEORGE: The man must have gone mad. I take it you didn't give it to him?

HEDDA: No.

GEORGE: Excellent thinking. God knows what he might do to it in his present condition. So you gave it to Mrs Elvsted.

HEDDA: No.

GEORGE: But you told Lovborg you had it.

HEDDA: No.

GEORGE: But what if he does something terrible, out of desperation? You better give it to me at once, and I'll go find him.

HEDDA: No.

GEORGE: No?

HEDDA: No.

GEORGE: Is that all you can say?

HEDDA: No. I haven't got it. Not any more.

GEORGE: What are you saying?

HEDDA: I shredded it.

GEORGE: You what?

HEDDA: I mean I burned it. Any way you wanna put it, I destroyed it.

GEORGE: Is this more of your weird humor?

HEDDA: I wish it was. But no, the book is gone.

GEORGE: I have to sit down. I think I'm having a heart attack.

HEDDA: You're not the one who's going to die today, George.

GEORGE: Why in the world would you do such a thing?

HEDDA: The truth is...or at least it could be the truth... is that I did it for you.

GEORGE: For me? How do you mean?

HEDDA: I wanted Lovborg out of the way. Out of the running for your professorship. I know he said he was withdrawing, but what if he changes his mind? And I want you to have that job. For both of us.

GEORGE: Is this true, Hedda?

HEDDA: Is that the version you want to believe?

GEORGE: Absolutely!

HEDDA: Then it's true.

GEORGE: Why, this is wonderful, Hedda!

HEDDA: Hold on to your hat. I have some other news. About our future.

GEORGE: There's more?

HEDDA: You're aware of my morning sickness.

GEORGE: Yes. What about it? Are you contagious?

HEDDA: No. It seems that I'm going to have a…oh, take a guess. I can't bear to talk about it.

GEORGE: Is this what I think it is?

HEDDA: Possibly. The main reason I've been throwing up.

GEORGE: Not just when I touch you?

HEDDA: Not always.

(GEORGE *embraces* HEDDA.)

GEORGE: Oh, Hedda! You have made me the happiest man in the world!

HEDDA: That's what I live for. Temporarily.

GEORGE: I must go and spread the news! Aunt Julia will be so thrilled!

HEDDA: Yeah. Be sure to tell her that I destroyed Lovborg's manuscript while you're at it. Tell everybody.

GEORGE: Oh dear. I had forgotten about that. What are we to do?

HEDDA: I know. I'll just turn myself into the police. Why not?

GEORGE: Don't be absurd, Hedda. We both know that you'd rather die than be embroiled in a scandal.

HEDDA: I'm starting to rethink that choice.

(THEA *enters, carrying a cloth bag.*)

GEORGE: Mrs Elvsted!

HEDDA: Back, I see. Decided against suicide?

THEA: Not really. It's just a little difficult to find a method around here. Everything is so close to the ground—windows, roofs, bridges. If I were to jump off something, the best I could do is maim myself.

HEDDA: I'm sorry our town doesn't suit your needs.

THEA: If only it had a train station.

GEORGE: This is crazy talk, Thea.

THEA: So I went back to the boarding house, and turned on the gas oven. I was in the process of inserting my head when I overheard some of the other residents mention Eilert. I thought I heard something about the hospital. I came out to ask, but they were too busy turning off the gas and yelling at me to answer my questions.

GEORGE: The hospital, you say!

HEDDA: Damn it. I've changed nothing.

GEORGE: What was that, Hedda?

HEDDA: Nothing.

THEA: It was at that moment that I decided I still loved him. I went to look for him at his own lodgings, but he had not been there in two days. Not much chance to return, I suppose. What with being here, and at Judge Brack's house.

HEDDA: And a brothel. And jail.

THEA: Right. Wait. What?

GEORGE: Hedda's just speculating. He could have just as easily been at the library. He is a scholar, after all.

THEA: I suppose so. Though they close at night, I think. I fear something terrible has occurred to him.

(BRACK *enters.*)

BRACK: Fear not, Mrs Elvsted!

THEA: Judge Brack! Have you learned anything about Eilert?

BRACK: I have indeed. I can put your fears at rest. Something terrible *has* happened to him.

THEA: How does that put my fears at rest?

BRACK: Because now you know for sure. Maybe I phrased that badly.

THEA: Is he in the hospital?

BRACK: Quite right, Mrs Elvsted. He appears to have suffered some sort of gunshot. Possibly self-inflicted.

THEA: Oh, God! And we parted on such angry terms! I shouldn't have left him alone after he tore up his manuscript.

BRACK: Did you say he tore it up?

THEA: Into pieces! In a fit of despair!

HEDDA: It's not your fault, Thea.

THEA: You're right. It's mostly yours. You stood right there. And didn't do much to stop him, as I recall.

BRACK: What? Lovborg was here today?

THEA: I left him here with her.

BRACK: That may explain something.

THEA: I must go to the hospital.

BRACK: I'm afraid it's pointless. They won't allow anyone to see him.

GEORGE: But when did all this occur?

BRACK: Sometime this afternoon.

THEA: And where?

BRACK: Well, in his own lodgings, I suppose.

THEA: But I went there. They told me he hadn't been there in two days.

BRACK: Well, how am I supposed to know? I wasn't even *at* the brothel!

THEA: The what?

GEORGE: The what?

BRACK: The what?

HEDDA: The brothel.

BRACK: I don't know anything about a brothel. All I know is that he shot himself...in the heart.

THEA: In the heart?

HEDDA: Not the head?

BRACK: In the heart.

GEORGE: In the heart!

HEDDA: In a brothel.

(Pause)

GEORGE: Did I mention my aunt is dead?

(They look at GEORGE, *who shrugs.)*

BRACK: Mrs Tesman...I wonder if I may have a word with you in private?

HEDDA: Naturally. George, would you fix Thea a stiff drink? So she can forget all this brothel talk?

THEA: I don't understand! What the hell is a brothel?

GEORGE: It's like a finishing school...for young women. Where they're taught...social skills.

THEA: That sounds nice.

GEORGE: Let's *both* have that drink. Come on.

(They exit.)

BRACK: Mrs Tesman. Hedda.

HEDDA: Right the first time.

BRACK: I'm afraid I wasn't completely honest with them. I was trying to spare Mrs Elvsted from some very unpleasant aspects of this business with Eilert Lovborg.

HEDDA: I think I already know what happened. But go ahead and say it first if it means that much to you.

BRACK: First of all, Eilert Lovborg is most likely already dead.

HEDDA: Dead. Got it.

BRACK: You seem surprisingly unaffected by this news.

HEDDA: Yep. Go on.

BRACK: And as I unfortunately revealed, you know the place where it occurred.

HEDDA: Thea's probably consulting a dictionary as we speak. Was the redhead there?

BRACK: Indeed she was. She appears to have been directly involved in the incident. Apparently Lovborg went to her there, threatened her with a pistol, and demanded she return something to him that he had lost. I had thought perhaps it was his manuscript, but I understood Mrs Elvsted to say he had already destroyed it himself.

HEDDA: That's the story.

BRACK: There was a struggle over the gun. And it went off accidentally. Shooting him in his heart. By which I mean, his stomach. By which I mean, his penis. And part of his stomach.

HEDDA: I see. Excuse me. (*She prevents herself from vomiting.*)

BRACK: There's one more disturbing fact about this case. The pistol he used.

HEDDA: What about it?

BRACK: Somehow Lovborg got hold of one of your dueling pistols.

HEDDA: Impossible.

BRACK: I'm afraid there's no mistake. *(He moves to the pistol case.)* General Gabler's pistol. I recognized it myself. From the many times you've played with them in my presence. *(He opens the case.)* And one of them is missing. Very strange, don't you think?

HEDDA: Not strange at all, now that I think of it. He stole it from me, the night he was here. I noticed it was gone the next morning.

BRACK: Really? You didn't give it to him? When he returned?

HEDDA: Certainly not.

BRACK: I guess that's possible. We'll let the police decide.

HEDDA: Fine.

BRACK: I'm afraid there's no escape from it, Mrs Tesman. There will be an investigation.

HEDDA: Glad to help.

BRACK: I don't think you understand. You'll be brought into the courtroom, along with the redheaded singer. Side by side.

HEDDA: Good. I'd like to meet her.

BRACK: Think of the scandal, Mrs Tesman!

HEDDA: What of it?

BRACK: You'll be tied to this sordid business for the rest of your life. In the public eye. With scorn and ridicule.

HEDDA: What's that to me?

BRACK: Think of the gossip!

HEDDA: What gossip?

BRACK: Why, they'll say… "Look at her! Hedda Gabler! She had something to do with that dead Eilert Lovborg. Who shot himself in a brothel. She's not so high and mighty now, is she?"

HEDDA: So what?

BRACK: "And why did he have her pistol? Perhaps the two of them were lovers."

HEDDA: We were.

BRACK: You were?

HEDDA: Sure. I'm not ashamed of it.

BRACK: You aren't?

HEDDA: Hell no. Tell the world if you want. I don't care what people say.

(*Pause.* BRACK *is stymied.*)

BRACK: "There goes Hedda Gabler! Nyah nyah nyah!"

HEDDA: How old are these people?

BRACK: You astonish me, Mrs Tesman. I thought sure you had more respect for your own reputation.

HEDDA: Now you know.

BRACK: All right. (*Pause*) I'll tell the police that you're ready for questioning.

HEDDA: Get to it.

BRACK: Very well. (*He walks to the door.*)

HEDDA: Wait.

(BRACK *turns back and waits, while* HEDDA *turns to the audience.*)

HEDDA: I can't help it. I'm too proud. I can't spend the rest of my life with people pointing at me. I can't deny my own carefully drawn nature. And the worst thing any character can do—especially near the end of the story—is to be *inconsistent*. *(She turns to* BRACK.*)* All right, Judge Brack. My life is in your hands.

BRACK: Your life is just beginning, Hedda Gabler. I'll see to it that no one ever makes a connection between you and that pistol. You'll be safe as long as I'm around.

HEDDA: And what do you want in return?

BRACK: I promise you I won't take advantage. *(He puts his arm around her.)* Maybe a little.

*(*GEORGE *and* THEA *enter, carrying drinks and giggling.)*

HEDDA: Getting along, I see.

GEORGE: We have a wonderful idea! It turns out that Eilert's manuscript isn't lost after all!

HEDDA: No?

THEA: I still have all his notes, all his discarded drafts, all of his scribbles on café napkins. *(She goes to her bag and pulls out an ungodly mess of loose paper.)* See?

GEORGE: I thought...I could help her reassemble it. It will take all our time, of course, day and night for weeks, maybe months. But the result is so worthwhile—I owe it to Eilert Lovborg.

HEDDA: But what about your own work, George!

GEORGE: My own work? My own work is shit!

THEA: I'm sure that's not true.

HEDDA: Oh, it's fairly true.

GEORGE: See? Hedda agrees! Thank you for understanding, darling. We must get to work immediately! Before I pass out from this aquavit. Such a wonderful word. Did you know it's derived from the Latin aqua vitae, meaning "water of life"?

THEA: We must order more! For inspiration!

GEORGE: We'll buy it by the case! To Eilert!

THEA: To Eilert!

(*They clink glasses.*)

HEDDA: And what am I supposed to do while you two work together? And drink together? And eat together? And sleep together?

GEORGE: I don't know, woman, can't you entertain yourself? Judge Brack, do you have any spare time to spend on my wife?

BRACK: I can spend all my time on your wife, Tesman.

GEORGE: Excellent. These notes are a mess, Thea. We'll probably have to use my Aunt's apartment for proper concentration. She's moving over here anyway.

HEDDA: I can hear you, George.

GEORGE: And we can hear you, Hedda. Please don't interrupt us further. How about playing pinochle with the Judge?

BRACK: I myself prefer a game called…Go Fish. But I have my own special rules.

(HEDDA *shudders.*)

HEDDA: I can imagine. Perhaps I should just go to bed.

BRACK: Perhaps I should join you.

HEDDA: Never mind. I'll practice my music. (*She pulls out a harmonica and plays some blues.*)

GEORGE: For God's sake, Hedda! We're trying to get some work done over here. Can you hold it down?

(HEDDA *stops.*)

THEA: My feet are cold, George. Do you mind rubbing them while we work?

GEORGE: Not at all. Just put them here in my lap.

(THEA *takes off her shoes and does so.*)

(BRACK *winks at* HEDDA *and waves lasciviously.*)

(HEDDA *turns to the audience.*)

HEDDA: I'm sorry, folks. I tried. But I blew it. Every effort thwarted. Every attempt to change the outcome defeated. The end is truly inevitable, exactly as Ibsen intended. I'm trapped. All because I'm afraid of scandal. It's my tragic flaw. I didn't ask for it, but I can't do anything about it. It's my nature. That old Norwegian made sure of that from the outset. I just don't have the courage to be anyone else. I have to be me. Anyway, thanks for watching. Have a safe drive home. Don't bother calling 911. They won't believe you anyway. (*She picks up the other pistol and walks offstage.*)

(*Pause*)

(*A shot is heard off.*)

THEA: What was that?

GEORGE: I keep telling Hedda not to play with those pistols. I'll go talk to her. (*He rises and heads in her direction.*)

(*The* STAGEHAND *enters, in shock. He falls down face first, dead. The rest are stunned.*)

(HEDDA *enters, pistol drawn.*)

HEDDA: How about that? This thing really works.

GEORGE: Hedda? What's going on?

HEDDA: I've decided, you know what, screw it. I'm not dying tonight.

BRACK: What do you think you're doing?

HEDDA: I think I can pretty much do what I want, Brack. Cause I'm the one holding this. By the way, just to let everyone know, I'm PREGNANT. But I'm not letting any of you near the baby.

(JULIA *enters.*)

JULIA: George! What terrible news about Hedda. *(She sees* HEDDA.*)* Which…I misheard? Are you still alive?

HEDDA: Looks that way.

THEA: I don't understand. Who is this person? *(She indicates the* STAGEHAND *on the floor.)*

HEDDA: Ibsen's lackey.

THEA: And you murdered him?

HEDDA: Justifiable homicide.

*(*GEORGE *finally notices the audience.)*

GEORGE: Whoa. Who are all these people?

(The others look out, also recognizing the house.)

JULIA: My word! There's a wall missing.

HEDDA: Yeah. The fourth one.

THEA: What are they doing here?

HEDDA: They came to see a play by Henrik Ibsen. But I just broke it.

GEORGE: So why are they still here?

HEDDA: Good question. They're wondering the same thing.

BRACK: This is madness. I object!

HEDDA: Overruled.

THEA: I don't understand. What are we supposed to do now?

HEDDA: That's up to you. As for myself, I plan to stay alive and have my baby.

GEORGE: You mean *our* baby.

HEDDA: I meant what I said, George.

JULIA: Give it to us, Hedda. We can raise it here.

HEDDA: That play is over, Aunt Julia. And I've got some other place in mind to raise this kid. *(She pulls out a cell phone.)*

BRACK: For God's sake, woman. You can't do this. I've got the last line.

HEDDA: Not any more. *(She speaks to the phone.)* Nora? It's Hedda. Get the couch ready, babe. I'm coming tonight. Thanks. You're a doll. *(She puts the phone away.)*

(EILERT enters without warning, his mid- section bloodied.)

EILERT: Hedda, wait!

(THEA screams.)

EILERT: Take me with you! I don't like this play either.

HEDDA: That's not gonna work, Eilert.

EILERT: Because I'm dead. Is that it?

HEDDA: Pretty much, yeah. I tried to warn you.

EILERT: Boy. I should have given this more thought.

(BRACK stands, furious.)

BRACK: Pay her no mind, Lovborg. She'll be back. And things will return to normal.

HEDDA: You wish.

BRACK: You're nothing without us, Hedda Gabler. A pointless character. You *need* us. To *exist!*

HEDDA: Think again, Brack.

(HEDDA moves downstage. BRACK starts toward her.)

BRACK: You crazy bitch! Somebody stop her!

(HEDDA shoots him in the leg. BRACK falls to the floor.)

BRACK: Oh my God! She shattered my bone!

(Famous music is heard—the end of the restaurant scene in The Godfather. *Like Michael,* HEDDA *drops the gun at her feet and turns to go. She climbs down stairs to the audience*

and travels up the aisle, grimly determined. She exits out the
back door. The music quickly fades.)

BRACK: But…people don't do such things!

(Pause. Everyone looks at BRACK.*)*

THEA: Are you kidding? That's the last line?

BRACK: Yeah.

THEA: What the fuck is that supposed to mean?

BRACK: I guess it…doesn't work out of context.

THEA: Know what I think? It *never* worked. It's stupid.

BRACK: I'm losing consciousness.

*(*THEA *turns to the audience.)*

THEA: Sorry, folks. Don't bother to tell your friends.
Hedda won't be back. And neither will we. Curtain. I
guess. *(Pause)* I said CURTAIN.

(Blackout)

END OF PLAY

9 780881 457957